THE LIFE ACTIONBOOK

Tools and Actions for Personal Development

STEVE ALVEST

CONTENTS

JOIN STORMSHOCK

Want to see secret blog posts, get free and discounted books, and get updated content? Join the StormShock e-mail list.

It's free. I'll keep your e-mail secret. Unsubscribe at any time.

Subscribe at www.smshock.com/list

INTRODUCTION

One of my tenets of writing is only to write what I would want to read for myself. Nobody is perfect. I know that I am far from perfect and have a lot of work to do. That is why I wrote this book. It is not a traditional self-improvement book. I won't stand on a pedestal and try to be your guru. I won't tell you what you should or shouldn't do. I won't try to advise strangers without knowing anything about their unique situations.

That said, I do want to help you. I want to help you as much as I want to help myself. Self-help books get a bad rap. When I was younger, I would always walk past the self-help section at bookstores thinking, "I don't need help. Those are books for people with problems." But as I got older, I realized that everyone has problems. Life itself is a game of solving problems. The self-help section of the bookstore is like the answer book that sat hidden in the first drawer of the teacher's desk in grade school. It turns out that those people in the self-help section at bookstores were the smart ones. They recognized their problems and decided to do something about them. That's a lot more than most people are willing to do. Most people let their problems be. They take the easy path, which is to do nothing.

We no longer call these books "self-help" books. People don't want to be helped. But they *do* want to improve themselves or develop their skills. So now we call them "self-improvement" or "personal development" books. Same thing, but with a friendlier connotation than "self-help." Their purpose remains the same—to provide answers to the problems that crop up in life.

This book doesn't have one-size-fits-all answers. I don't know what your situation is, so I can't point you to a particular solution. In this book, I show you many possible solutions. It's your job to choose the ones that may work for you and apply them to your life.

This book is a workbook (of sorts) for finding the areas for improvement in your life and fixing them. Each chapter discusses one area of life. You will take a short self-assessment quiz. If that area of your life is not up to par, the rest of the chapter will provide ideas for habits, hacks, tools, supplements, and resources that you can use to improve yourself.

While I want to refrain from giving advice where possible,

I do have one crucial piece of wisdom that everyone should follow. Adopt a *kaizen* approach to life. Kaizen is the Japanese word for "improvement." When used in a business context, it refers to the continuous improvement of all aspects of the company including processes, employees, and even the CEO. You should be continuously improving your life. Each day you wake up is another opportunity to be a better person than you were yesterday. It's another chance to eat better, interact with others better, perform better, *live better*.

~

WHO ARE YOU? (AND WHY SHOULD I LISTEN TO YOU?)

I grew up in a middle-class, suburban American family. My grades were okay in school, but I was never exceptional. I went to college and graduated. Then I got married and worked a stable government job for ten years. Somewhere in between, we bought a house and had three kids. Thus far, I've lived a successful life with no regrets.

But something was still missing. I wasn't passionate about what I was doing. I started thinking, "so do I just keep doing this for the next 30 years and then retire?"

When I was working my 9-5 job, I began the habit of reading popular non-fiction books on my daily Metro commutes to and from work. In 2011, I came across a book that changed my mindset and my life. The book was *The 4-*

Hour Workweek, by Timothy Ferriss. It wasn't so much the content of the book that changed my life, but the subject matter that intrigued me. I found a new passion. That passion was what Ferriss called "lifestyle design."

Lifestyle design is a new breed of self-improvement. You start with the end in mind. What kind of life do you want to live ten years from now? Once you know that, you can figure out what you need to do to get there.

After reading hundreds of books related to redesigning my life, I quit my job in 2016 to set my plans in motion. I began focusing less on the reading and more on the actions. This book is a collection of actions. Each one of them has worked for someone in the past. It might not work for you, but it is worth trying. I wrote this book for myself so that I could have my notes on actionable items all in one place. I hope it is useful to you as well. Let's take action together.

~

AN ACTIONBOOK

The term "workbook" calls to mind a physical book with thin gray pages, questions, and lots of lines for you to write on. The book you're holding is most likely an ebook or a small physical paperback. There are no lines in it. It's not a workbook.

Think of this book as an "actionbook." Instead of reading through it while working, I want you to read it while taking actions. If you're reading a physical copy, feel free to write in it, highlight passages, put sticky notes in it, or mangle its pages. If it's the electronic version you're reading, have a notebook handy, so you can take notes or doodle while you read. Make a note of which sections you completed or skipped. Mark which suggestions you've tried. Did they succeed or did they not work out for you?

The important thing is to take action. Don't read this book and put it away without having made any changes in your life. I assure you, there is much better literature out there than this book. Try the various suggestions. Some of them will drastically improve your life. But they won't have any effect if you don't take action.

~

DISCLAIMER

You are in control of your own life. You make decisions every day that affect your future well-being. As mentioned before, this is not a book of advice. It is a book of ideas and suggestions for things you can try. I am not a doctor, lawyer, or accountant. I am a researcher and author. While I go to great lengths to ensure that the information in this book is factual and current, in the end, any action you take is your decision.

Every person is different. Starting a new jogging habit might be helpful for most people, but it may be dangerous to some people with heart conditions. Drinking more green tea may help most people, but may be hazardous to people with liver disease. Use your judgment when making lifestyle changes. When in doubt, consult a professional. There is no one-size-fits-all solution when it comes to life changes.

I gleaned most of the content in this book from other sources. I spent countless hours reading, researching, and trying things so I could curate and compile the best material for this book. All I'm doing is reporting on what better-qualified people are saying. Sometimes I put two and two together and form conclusions or offer personal insights. On those occasions, I try to make it obvious. Read this book as a summary of much of the information that's out there. Try the things that look safe for you, but skip over any suggestions that you're wary of.

∼

HABITS

Your success, your health, your relationships, and everything else that defines your life are the product of your habits. Everything you do and every decision you make is based on your habits. Eating dinner is a habit. Hitting the snooze button on your alarm clock in the morning is a habit. Even spontaneously deciding to take an alternate route to work might come from a broader habit of mixing things up every once in awhile.

Our brains are continually sensing the environment and coming to logical conclusions about how the world works. In our subconscious minds, we form truths and mental models based on all our past experiences. As babies, we felt hungry, so we cried, and we were fed. From that point, we cried whenever we wanted food. It was a truth to us, until one day it didn't work. We cried, and we weren't fed. The thing we knew to be true was proven untrue, so we had to find a new solution. Perhaps it was a pat of the tummy, or reaching for a bottle, or saying "eat." Once we see a new solution, then we form a new truth to base future habits upon.

We use our knowledge of how the world works to form habits. Our habits influence every decision. And every decision we make affects the outcomes in our lives. That is why to change our lives we must change our habits. We can't change how the world works, but we can change our habits.

Good and Bad Habits

We all have both good and bad habits. It's obvious that we all want to have more good habits and drop the bad ones. But it's not easy to get rid of bad habits. In fact, it can be almost impossible.

One way to get rid of bad habits is to replace them with good practices. It can be too difficult to simply stop doing a bad habit. You need something to fill the void. If you can find a good habit that takes the same amount of time and has similar benefits of the bad one, you can swap the bad habit for the good habit. For example, if you have the bad habit of talking on your phone while driving, you can start listening to podcasts while driving instead. Both activities fill the same amount of time while you are driving. And both actions have similar benefits of filling your driving time with something worthwhile.

While some people may have succeeded in drastically changing their lives in a short amount of time, most people fail at "cold turkey" solutions. Realize that most habits are not all or nothing. If you're quitting smoking, getting down to five cigarettes a day is better than a pack a day. If you're starting a jogging habit, getting outside and running once a week is better than none at all. Set your habit goals, but don't let setbacks derail you. Do the best you can. Even if you fail most of the time with a few minor successes, it's still better than not even trying.

One Habit at a Time

Many people make the mistake of trying to change too much at once. It often occurs at the beginning of a new year when people attempt to reinvent themselves. They want to lose weight, go vegan, make more money, and quit smoking all at the same time. And they end in catastrophic failure after three days.

Don't try to change more than one aspect of your life at once. It takes time to turn a lone action into a daily habit. It takes at least a couple weeks to develop a new habit. I suggest developing one new habit each month. Create a 30-day challenge for yourself. At the beginning of each month, decide on one aspect of your life you want to change. Then focus on that single issue for the entire month.

Using a series of 30-day challenges to change your life turns it into a game. You either succeed or fail in each challenge. The habit is either created or not. And the challenge only lasts a month. It is a huge accomplishment if you succeed, but still beneficial even if you fail. You might not achieve your goal, but you will make more progress than if you had not tried at all. Because the experiment is limited to a month, you can learn from it and move on. Each new month gives you the opportunity to start another exciting challenge. Do a year of 30-day challenges. It will transform and your life.

Anchors and Triggers

Another common problem people have when starting a new habit is remembering to do it each day. Sometimes people have trouble fitting a new routine into their busy schedules. The solution is anchoring.

To anchor a habit, you attach it to an existing routine. For example, if you want to build a habit of doing thirty push-ups every day, you can anchor it to your daily shower. Resolve to do thirty push-ups before you get in the shower. Your daily shower is already an established habit, so you will not forget to do it. If you make doing push-ups part of your shower routine, you will remember to do them.

Triggers are like anchors but tend to apply to bad habits instead of good ones. A trigger is something that makes your bad practices more likely to happen. Your location, time, emotional state, people around you, and things you're doing can all trigger bad habits. It's harder to avoid drinking alcohol when you're sitting at the bar. It's easier to overeat when you're at a buffet. It becomes much more difficult to avoid wasting time on the internet once you start checking your social media accounts. Identify the triggers for your bad habits and avoid them. Better yet, preempt them with good habits.

Once you've identified a trigger for a bad habit, think about what triggered the trigger. For example, if you're trying to quit soda and eating greasy foods makes you feel like drinking it, think about what happens before you eat greasy foods. If hunger between meals causes you to eat greasy foods, try anchoring some good habits to your mealtimes, so you don't get hungry before the next meal. Maybe you can make a habit of drinking a full glass of water after each meal. Or eat more protein during mealtimes. Or after each meal, do something good for yourself that doesn't allow you to take a snack break before the next meal (like going to the library to study after lunch). Just make sure you're attacking the root of the problem and not the symptoms.

Accountability

Sometimes the best way to stick with your goals is to tell others about them. If you tell everybody that you will start riding your bike to work every day, you are more likely to do it. Once other people know your goals, you will feel a sense of embarrassment if you fail to achieve them. The threat of humiliation can be a strong motivator.

The most reliable form of accountability is personal accountability with another person. Tell a friend about your goals. The closer your relationship with the person, the stronger your motivation will be. Tell your spouse, roommates, or best friend. You can even hire someone to hold you accountable. Simply pay someone to check in on you daily to make sure you're working towards your goal.

There are also ways to hold yourself accountable online. Many apps can help you build habits.

- Coach.me (www.coach.me) is a social media habit app where you can add friends, send messages, and ask questions. You choose the habits you want to build and check in whenever you complete it. You can also connect with a coach to provide guidance and motivation.
- 21habit (www.21habit.com) lets you set a goal and form a habit in twenty-one days.
- Strides (www.stridesapp.com) helps you set SMART goals. Set Specific, Measurable, Achievable, Relevant, and Timely goals and track your progress.
- DietBet (www.dietbet.com) makes a game out of losing weight. You put real money into a virtual pot. Send "before" pictures showing your current weight. Then you have 28 days to lose 4% of your

body weight. If you succeed, you split the pot with the other winners. Otherwise, you lose the money.

While online accountability may be the weakest form, it can still be useful. The main strength of accountability apps is gamification. They turn habit formation into a game by encouraging you to check in every day and comparing you to others.

~

TYPES OF FIXES

While changing your habits is the best long-term solution to your problems, there are other types of fixes. Be aware that there are no real shortcuts in life. Each chapter of this book offers four additional classes of solutions: hacks, supplements, tools, and resources.

Hacks

You can think of hacks as short-term solutions. Apply them as a quick fix to a problem. There are often negative consequences for continually using the same hacks over an extended period. For example, downing a cup of coffee and taking a short nap is one way to wake yourself up if you only got four hours of sleep the night before. But, if you get four hours of sleep every night, you cannot rely on these caffeine naps for more than a few days at a time. You first need to fix the bad habit of sleeping too little.

Supplements

Supplements are a "magic pill" solution to your problems. They are herbal remedies, over-the-counter medicines, and specialty foods that can help your situation. Like hacks, I don't recommend taking supplements as a long-term solution to your problems. Herbal remedies are a form of drug that can have severe side-effects if taken long-term or in large quantities. Even many foods can have side-effects if you go too far with consumption. As always, discuss any dietary changes you want to make with your doctor.

Tools

Tools are gadgets and products you can buy to help you with your goals. If you have some money to spend on improving your life, these tools can make things easier. Abraham Lincoln once said, "Give me six hours to chop down a tree, and I will spend the first four sharpening the ax." When you have a big task ahead of you, having the right tools can mean the difference between success and failure. Try out whatever means you can afford. Confidently walk into your tasks carrying a sharp ax.

Resources

Finally, I've included resources for further reading. This book is just a brief overview of the many facets of self-improvement. There are books, videos, websites, and podcasts that explore the subjects in greater detail. If you want to go deeper into a particular topic, check out the resources at the end of each chapter.

~

HOW TO READ THIS BOOK

This book is not your typical personal development book. You should not read it from the beginning to end. It doesn't have pep-talks or motivational stories. It won't tell you what to do. This is a book of ideas for things you can try.

Each chapter starts with a quiz to assess your level of mastery on a topic. If you've already mastered the subject of the section, you should skip it. There is no use in fixing something that's not broken. If there is much room for improvement, then read through the suggestions and take action. Choose one tip and try it. For those topics that you haven't mastered yet, but aren't entirely failing at, skip them for now and revisit them after you've made one pass through the book. Discover your weaknesses first, then find ways to improve in those areas.

Realize that everyone is different. Something that is easy for you may be difficult for someone else. If you come across an exercise that looks too challenging for you to try, skip it and move on to the next one. The exercises are only suggestions of things you can try. They are not directives for what you should or should not do. Not every activity will work for you.

Engage in active reading. Keep a notepad next to you as you read. Whenever something catches your attention or strikes you as a good idea to try, write it in your notes. Writing helps you remember and gets your mind thinking down a path of action. It is especially important to write down your answers to the questions at the beginning of each chapter. Remember, this is an actionbook for you to take action. It is not meant to read like a novel.

～

DETAILS

This book covers nine broad personal development topics: mindset, sleep, time management, career, diet, fitness, social skills, organization, and personal finances. For each subject, I give you several ideas for how you can improve that area of your life. Note that each list of ideas is just the tip of a colossal iceberg of knowledge. There are hundreds of ways you can approach a problem. I only give you a couple dozen. But the ideas you find in this book will at least get you thinking about some of the possibilities.

Every idea given here includes a summary. Due to the space constraints of this book, the summary is often not enough information to make informed decisions. Each idea has enough information to get you started, but you should do due diligence to ensure that the action is right for you. Get more detailed information by searching the internet. For ideas that involve physical movement or ingesting things, be sure to consult your doctor. For ideas concerning legal aspects, ask your lawyer when in doubt. I know we already discussed this in the disclaimer section, but it's important to repeat. When in doubt about anything in this book, dig deeper by doing your own research and consulting experts.

Chapter One

MINDSET

It's hard to find success when your head is a mess. You might be your own worst enemy. But once you're at peace with your mind, everything will fall into place. Why? Because your mental state is what drives all your actions. And your life can only improve through action.

The questions in this quiz are subjective. Spend some time thinking about each one. Be honest with yourself.

Question 1: Do you know your purpose in life?

Your answer:

- No. Struggling through life every day seems meaningless: 0 points.
- Maybe. I enjoy what I do, but I'm not sure I've found my life purpose yet: 1 point.
- Yes: 2 points.

Question 2: How anxious, stressed, and mentally overwhelmed are you?

Your answer:

- I'm mentally overwhelmed to the point that I have trouble sleeping because I can't turn off my thoughts: 0 points.
- I often feel stressed or anxious: 1 point.
- I'm laid-back and find it easy to stay calm: 2 points.

Question 3: How much control do you have over your actions?

Your answer:

- I turn to distractions, alcohol, or other harmful compulsions to relax my mind each day: 0 points.
- I have trouble reaching my goals because of distractions or self-sabotage: 1 point.
- I have no trouble setting goals and succeeding: 2 points.

Add up all your points and see how you fared.

- 0-2 points: read this chapter now.
- 3-4 points: come back to this chapter later.
- 5-6 points: skip this chapter, you're good.

∽

THE IMPORTANCE OF MINDSET

Attitude is everything. Mindset is everything. For you to be successful, your thoughts need to be organized. You need to understand yourself.

Many people view meditation as superstitious new age woo with no basis in science. But the practice actually goes back to the beginning of human history. Meditation is not just sitting with your legs crossed, eyes closed, and humming "om." You can think of any practice of focusing on your mind as a form of meditation. It might be visualization, sitting in silence, gratefulness, prayer, or even doing yard work while immersed in deep thought.

If you want to be successful, you need to think like a successful person. When you start thinking like somebody who is successful, everything else will fall into place. Success begins with mindset.

A good mindset to have is Stoicism. Stoicism is all about not worrying about things that you can't change. Some things are out of your control. Worrying about those things will get you nowhere. Instead, you should occupy your mind only with things that you do have control over. Let go and accept anything that is out of your control.

Success is all about being able to conquer the challenges you face to reach the goals you set for yourself. A good mindset is the difference between solving every unpredictable challenge you encounter, or breaking.

~

MEDITATION

At the broadest level, meditation is any practice that clears the mind of undesired thoughts. When most people think of meditation, they think of someone sitting in a lotus position, eyes closed, and in deep thought. But there are so many ways you can meditate.

Sound. In general, you perform meditation in silence. But, some forms of meditation encourage saying mantras. A mantra is something you chant over and over again to get your mind into a meditative state. Some people also like to have external soothing sounds or sounds of nature around them as they meditate.

Pose. The primary consideration for the pose is that you are comfortable while meditating. The classic meditation pose is sitting with your legs crossed in a lotus position, but you can also sit in a chair or even stand. Most practitioners advise against laying down because it's too easy to fall asleep that way. Another option is to immerse yourself in thought while walking or doing a repetitive task. Whatever you choose, make sure you are comfortable and it is safe to "zone out" for the duration of your meditation.

Breath. How you breathe is vital to the meditation practice. Breathing helps you relax and channel your energy. There are many techniques for meditative breathing, but most involve taking slow deep breaths. The easiest way to regulate your breathing is by counting in your head. Again, there are many variations, but you can start with this: breathe in for 5 seconds, then breathe out for 7 seconds.

Thought. Meditation is useful for clearing your mind of unwanted thoughts. Think of nothing as you meditate. It's much harder than it sounds, especially if you are used to keeping busy. If you have trouble, try concentrating on your breathing. Or you can repeat a nonsense word (a mantra) in your head to prevent you from thinking of other things. As you meditate, try to gain an awareness of your body. How does your chair feel against your back? Do you feel pain anywhere in your body? What are your five senses telling you as you wait in silence?

Time. An old Buddhist saying goes, "You should sit in meditation for 20 minutes a day. Unless you're too busy, then you should sit for an hour." It sounds like a paradox, but there is an important truth in it. The people who need meditation the most are the ones who think they have no time for it. If you've never meditated before, start with five minutes. Set a timer and zone out. Adjust your future sessions based on what you learn during your five-minute experiment.

Mindset Action #1: Incorporate meditation into your daily routine. Devote a minimum of ten minutes a day to meditation practice.

∼

PURPOSE

What is the meaning of your life? What drives you to get out of bed each morning? Why do you do the job you do? What makes you happiest? Where do you want to be in life ten years from now?

Success is fleeting if you don't have answers to these questions yet. Some people get lucky and make a fortune before understanding themselves. But that kind of success is different from the kind you find when you know yourself.

Often, the people who get lucky don't know how to hold onto their fortune, or they can't appreciate it. If you understand yourself and your desires and wants and work towards your goals, the feeling is much more satisfactory and lasting. That is because money is not what drives all of us. Some people have a lot of money, but the money is not what makes them happy. You need to understand yourself and what makes you happy.

One way to understand what makes you happy is to write down your thoughts. Keep a journal and write in it every day. Write whatever comes to your head. Don't edit what you write. Let the words flow as they come to you. Try to tap into your subconscious and write without any regard for whether your words make sense or are politically correct or not. Nobody will read it except for you.

Mindset Action #2: Every day, write your thoughts in a journal.

Once you have a sense of what drives you and what makes you happy, it is time to set your life goals. Everybody will die someday, and your purpose in life should be to have no regrets when you do die. Every action you take should be in the direction of your goals or a constant drive for improvement. In the end, nothing in this world matters to you except for your final thoughts as you lay on your deathbed.

. . .

Mindset Action #3: Write down your life goals. Do you have regrets? What can you do to rid your mind of those regrets?

∽

PROGRAMMING YOUR BRAIN

You are what you think. If you think you are worthless, then you are worthless. If you believe you are successful, then you are successful. If you think you're happy, then you are happy. Each person has their own mind. Each mind creates its own reality.

Your mind is more powerful than you think. Whatever you truly believe becomes your own reality, unless it clashes with somebody else's reality. You can't control what other people think, but you have full control over your thoughts.

There are ways to program your brain to think in specific ways that manifest your goals. One such away is affirmations. Affirmations are things that you say to yourself over and over again. If you say something to yourself enough, then you eventually believe it. Believing something does not make it real, but it does make you more aware of opportunities to make it come true.

Mindset Action #4: What do you want more than anything

else? Make it an affirmation. If you want to be a millionaire, affirm to yourself several times a day, "I will be a millionaire by the end of this year. I am working hard to make money."

Another way to program your brain is through visualization. Visualization is like affirmations because you're repeating something in your head so that you will believe it. With affirmations you're repeating words, while with visualization you are repeating images in your head. Close your eyes and visualize yourself completing your goals. When you can see yourself accomplishing your goals, you are much more likely to succeed.

Mindset Action #5: At least once a day, close your eyes and visualize yourself succeeding in your goals. Visualize with as much detail as possible.

A more direct way of programming your brain involves feeding your mind with a steady diet of inspirational and educational content. Just as you are what you eat, you are what you watch and read. There is a lot of junk content out there. Make sure that the content you consume is worthwhile. You can never get back a wasted hour of your time.

• • •

Mindset Action #6: Think about all the content you consume each day, such as news, social media, and television. Is there better content you can consume instead?

Finally, it is crucial to surround yourself with positivity. When you have a lot of negativity around you, things look bleaker and more impossible. It is hard to do things when a fog of doubt surrounds you. Try to cut out the negativity in your life and seek out the positive.

Mindset Action #7: Do you come in contact with negativity in your life? Is there anything you can do to replace it with something positive?

~

MINDFULNESS

You are an extraordinarily lucky person. You might not feel that way, but you are. Think about all the good things in your life. Sure, there are plenty of places where your life can improve. But you have many good things going for you that other people don't have.

Don't take anything for granted. If you have a sense of gratefulness for the things that you have, you are much more likely to be happy when you reach your goals. People who are not grateful are never happy. Because they don't practice gratefulness now, they won't practice gratefulness in the future when they have even more good things.

Mindset Action #8: What are you grateful for? At least once a day, take a moment to relish in happiness for what you have.

Gratefulness is intertwined with mindfulness. You need to be mindful of the things you have to be grateful for them. Mindfulness is a simple concept. You practice mindfulness by ridding your life of distractions. When you are not distracted, you can focus on the most important thing. You can focus on one thing at a time. That consistent focus is mindfulness.

Be mindful of everything that you do. While you are doing something, don't think of other things. Don't think about what you're going to do next. Don't think about what you did earlier. Just focus on the task at hand.

If a thought comes up while you are doing a task, write it down and continue doing your task. Always stay in the present because there is nothing you can do about the past and we are terrible predictors of the future.

Mindset Action #9: Do one thing at a time. Be present while you do each thing.

~

HACKS

There are many little things you can do now to make yourself calmer and more in control. Here are a few things you can try.

Mindset Action #10: Don't waste time deciding things that don't matter towards your goals. Steve Jobs famously wore only black turtlenecks. He didn't have to waste mental energy every day deciding what to wear. Focus on the things that matter in your life. Don't spend too much time on the things that don't.

Mindset Action #11: Try deep breathing. Take a five-minute break. Close your eyes and spend those five minutes concentrating on your breath. Breathe in for five seconds. Exhale a little bit slower and less forcefully for seven seconds.

Mindset Action #12: Avoid all technology for the first hour of every morning. Keep your phone and computer off. Use the time to read, write, meditate, or reflect on the day ahead.

. . .

Mindset Action #13: Thank someone each day. Put gratefulness into practice by thanking at least one person every day. You can give them a hand-written note, give them a call, text them, or thank them in person.

Mindset Action #14: Take a walk. We often lose sight of the simple things in our hectic lives. Schedule a daily walk. Having a regular walking habit allows you to get some sun, exercise, and lifts your mood. There are many ways to go about it, depending on what you want to get out of it. You can walk in silence and experience the environment around you, or you can listen to music or podcasts. You can walk alone or with your dog. You can walk fast or slow. Do what feels natural to you.

Mindset Action #15: Start your day grateful. Whenever you wake from sleep, say "thank you" in your head. Think of the things or people you are grateful for and say "thank you."

Mindset Action #16: Exercise. Get the blood flowing and energy levels up. Do a few minutes of yoga. Go for a jog. Run out the door and sprint for a minute. Drop down and do twenty push-ups. It doesn't have to take a lot of time or effort.

· · ·

Mindset Action #17: Write every day. As writer Anne Lamott advises, write one crappy page a day. Write whatever is on your mind. Just brain dump and get it all out of your head. Then you can shred the page.

Mindset Action #18: Say a prayer. You don't even have to be religious to say prayers. Just tell yourself what you want. It helps move your unconscious desires into consciousness. When thoughts reach consciousness, you are more likely to turn them into reality.

Mindset Action #19: Craft an evening routine. Quiet your mind before you sleep. You might read fiction before bed, or write in your journal. You might pray, or watch some television. Do the same thing every night before you sleep. It will train your mind to know when it is time to end your day.

Mindset Action #20: Make your bed in the morning. When you make your bed, you accomplish something. It's an early win that boosts your confidence for the rest of the day.

∽

SUPPLEMENTS

People have long used psychedelic drugs to give themselves otherworldly experiences. Most are illegal, so I cannot recommend them here. I have also never tried any for myself. Some are legal, but I will not recommend them because they can be dangerous when used without medical supervision. Instead, we will explore other, less hazardous supplements that can affect your thinking, creativity, and mood.

Mindset Action #21: Take vitamins. B vitamins including B_6, B_1, and B_3 help stabilize the body's lactate levels to reduce the chance of anxiety attacks. Large doses of vitamin C creates a tranquilizing effect that decreases anxiety. Vitamin E helps transport oxygen to the brain and thereby helps your body cope with stress.

Mindset Action #22: Try a supplement to boost your creativity. Aniracetam activates parts of the brain responsible for creativity. Choline increases blood flow to the brain. Aniracetam is often taken alongside a choline source (such as centrophenoxine) to improve creative problem-solving abilities. Piracetam is also part of the racetam family of nootropics. It increases communication between the two halves of the brain and has fewer known side effects. Researchers have shown that L-Tyrosine improves some creative thinking skills.

Mindset Action #23: Promote lucid dreaming. A lucid dream is a dream in which you are aware you are dreaming. Not only that, but you also have some control over your actions during your dreams. It allows you to have new experiences while you sleep, similar to hallucination. Huperzine-A is one supplement that increases the likelihood of lucid dreaming. It helps your brain keep access to your memories when you sleep, thus promoting lucid dreams. Dimethylaminoethanol (also known as DMAE or Deanol) is another supplement that aids in lucid dreaming. It is a naturally occurring compound in the brain that increases visualization activity in the brain. It also causes you to wake up in the middle of deep REM sleep without sacrificing your sleep quality. The combined effects of increased visualization and waking during deep sleep make DMAE an excellent supplement for lucid dreaming.

~

TOOLS

It doesn't cost money to set your mind straight. However, if you like having extra guidance or just like playing with new toys, you can check out some of these tools.

. . .

Mindset Action #24: Create a vision board. It's a place where you can pin up images that represent your dreams for the future. Put the board in your work area or somewhere where you can see it every day, especially while you visualize and meditate. You can also create a virtual vision board with Pinterest (www.pinterest.com).

Mindset Action #25: Keep a daily journal. Write about anything. The point is to write whatever is on your mind every day to get it out of your head. The DayOne app (www.dayoneapp.com) is an excellent choice for journaling on your mobile device. If you don't like the idea of typing on your mobile device, try recording your thoughts with a voice-to-text feature on your device.

Mindset Action #26: Try a meditation app. If you've never meditated before, you can download a free meditation app to guide you through the process. Headspace (www.headspace.com) and Oak (www.oakmeditation.com) are two meditation apps you can try.

Mindset Action #27: Draw on a Buddha Board (www.buddhaboard.com). The Buddha Board is a canvas that you paint on with water. As the water dries, your drawings disappear. It encourages you to be creative and value the present.

Mindset Action #28: Try Muse (www.choosemuse.com). Muse is a brain-sensing headband that tracks your brainwaves as you meditate. It records your brain activity data as you meditate so you can measure the effectiveness of your meditation sessions.

~

RESOURCES

Mindset Action #29: Listen to podcasts.

- Aubrey Marcus Podcast. Aubrey Marcus talks with top performers to bring forward the lessons learned from triumph and disaster.
- Inspirational Living (www.livinghour.org). Inspirational books and essays are adapted to motivate your mind, body, and spirit.
- Mind Body Musings Podcast. Maddy Moon offers guidance for women who want to stop overthinking, and start living with more trust, intuition, and flow.
- MindSet by Design. Andy Murphy interviews

world-class performers to find out what gives them a competitive edge.

Mindset Action #30: Visit blogs and websites to learn more about mindset and meditation.

- Zen Habits (www.zenhabits.net) is about finding simplicity and mindfulness in the daily chaos of our lives.
- Marc and Angel Hack Life (www. marcandangel.com) gives you the tools to identify and transform the limiting beliefs that keep you stuck.
- Transcendental Meditation (www.tm.org) is a technique for inner peace and wellness used by many famous people.
- Vipassanā (www.vipassana.com) is a form of mindfulness meditation developed in the Buddhist tradition.

Mindset Action #31: Read books on mindset.

- *Meditations*, by Marcus Aurelius.

- *Letters from a Stoic: Epistulae Morales AD Lucilium,* by Lucius Annaeus Seneca.
- *The Obstacle Is the Way: The Timeless Art of Turning Trials into Triumph,* by Ryan Holiday.
- *Essentialism: The Disciplined Pursuit of Less,* by Greg McKeown.
- *Declutter Your Mind: How to Stop Worrying, Relieve Anxiety, and Eliminate Negative Thinking,* by S.J. Scott and Barrie Davenport.

Chapter Two

SLEEP

Question 1: How long were you laying in bed with your eyes closed last night?

Your answer:

- Fewer than 6 hours: 0 points.
- 6-7.5 hours: 1 point.
- 8+ hours: 2 points.

You probably noticed the awkward way I phrased the question. That's because sleep is hard to quantify. While the length of rest is significant, quality of sleep can make a difference. Someone who tossed and turned for eight hours may feel worse than someone who had a deep sleep for six hours. But I've found that even if I can't sleep, keeping my eyes closed and trying to think of nothing (i.e., meditation) is almost as effective as sleep itself.

Most people need somewhere between seven and eight hours of sleep each night. It can vary by many factors including genetics and quality of sleep.

Question 2: How do you feel when you wake up?

Your answer:

- It's hard to get out of bed: 0 points.
- Groggy: 1 point.
- Ready to seize the day: 2 points.

How you feel when you wake up is an indication of sleep quality. If you have poor sleep quality, changing your bedtime routines may help.

Question 3: How often do you feel sleepy during the day?

· · ·

Your answer:

- I'm always sleepy: 0 points.
- I get sleepy once or twice during the day: 1 point.
- I'm energetic and awake from sunrise until sunset: 2 points.

If you feel sleepy during the day, you probably did not get enough quality sleep the night before. Sometimes your daytime habits may also make you feel drowsy. Not getting enough sunlight, overeating, or exhausting yourself may make you tired before bedtime.

Add up all your points and see how you fared:

- 0-2 points: read this chapter now.
- 3-4 points: come back to this section later.
- 5-6 points: skip this chapter, you're good.

∽

THE IMPORTANCE OF SLEEP

On its face, sleep is a massive waste of time. We spend several hours a day doing nothing. It's a third of our lives lying prone with our eyes closed. It's no wonder why many people try to reduce the amount of time they sleep.

But when we get too little sleep, bad things happen. We look older, become irritable, and make more mistakes. Our health declines and we get sick more often. We become less productive.

The benefits of sleep are many. Your skin looks more youthful, your hormones balance, and you lose weight faster. Your brain cleanses the toxins. Your body purges inflammation and recharges your immune system. You focus better, feel better, and have more energy.

It is tempting to sacrifice sleep for working another couple hours or getting a few more things done around the house. It's not worth it. When you sacrifice sleep, you're not gaining hours of productive time. You're taking it away from your future. Sleep debt is real. You may gain a couple of hours of productive time by sleeping later tonight, but you will be tired tomorrow. In fact, your productivity tomorrow will drop and reverse any gains you made the night before. You can't cheat time.

Sleep is a critical natural process. Getting too little will erase any productivity gained from sacrificing it in the past. A lack of sleep affects not only your productivity, but it also impairs your memory, creativity, and judgment. People become irritable and cranky. People who get irregular sleep have an increased risk of several mental illnesses including schizophrenia, depression, and bipolar disorder. The effects are also physical because sleep deprivation lowers your immune system and increases your chances of obesity.

Sleep Action #1: Starting today, keep a sleep log. Record what time you go to bed and what time you get up. Rate your quality of sleep. Take note of any naps you take throughout the day. Track your sleep habits for at least a week.

~

TIME

If you want to improve your sleep, the first thing you need to do is take it seriously. It is one of the most important things you do each day. A good night's sleep lays the foundation for everything you do after you wake up. It makes sense to make it a priority.

Schedule your sleep time beforehand. Start by deciding for yourself how many hours of sleep you need. It can vary between different people depending on many factors including genetics. Most people need somewhere between 7-9 hours of sleep each night.

Next, determine when you need to wake up. Count back the number of hours you need to sleep. For example, if you need eight hours of sleep and must wake up by 7 AM, you will count back eight hours from 7 AM to 11 PM. 11 PM is the time you need to be in bed. It is typically easier to set a regular waking time than it is to establish a consistent bedtime.

When deciding your sleep times, it helps to look at when sunrise and sunset occur. It varies depending on location and time of year. Get to bed within a few hours of sunset and try not to sleep past sunrise. The natural cycles of sunlight and darkness affect your hormone levels and can make sleeping difficult if you sleep at unnatural times.

Most people sleep in cycles of 90 minutes. Every 90 minutes, you wake, shift position in your bed, get up to use the bathroom, or otherwise awaken from deep slumber. It makes sense to plan your sleep in multiples of 90 minutes: 1:30, 3:00, 4:30, 6:00, 7:30, 9:00. Add the approximate amount of time it takes you to fall asleep. For example, if it takes you ten minutes to fall asleep, it would be better for you to be lying in bed for 6 hours and 10 minutes than for 7 hours. Getting interrupted in the middle of a deep sleep cycle will make you feel groggy.

Sleep Action #2: Block off your sleep times on your calendar once you've determined your bedtimes and waking times. Schedule your sleep like you would any other important activity. And remember: don't be late for your appointments.

∽

YOUR MIND

Often what keeps people awake at night is their own racing minds. To fall asleep, you must first turn off your conscious mind so your subconscious can take over. That involves calming your mind. There are several techniques you can try as you lay in bed struggling to fall asleep: meditation, gratitude, and breathing.

Meditation is the act of calming your mind. It often gets dismissed as woo-woo New Age stuff. But the fact is, it has been a useful tool for thousands of years. There's no harm in giving it a try, and you might be surprised by how helpful it can be.

Sleep Action #3: When you're trying to fall asleep, lay in bed and close your eyes. Try to think about nothing. Or, if that's too difficult, concentrate on your breathing. Whenever a thought enters your head, let go of it in your mind and watch it drift away.

Gratitude is like meditation, but instead of clearing your head, you fill it with good thoughts. By thinking about the positive, you push the negative worries out of mind.

Sleep Action #4: As you lay in bed, reflect on all the good things that happened during the day. Which people are you lucky to have in your life? Who helped you? What things do you have in life that others don't?

When you fall asleep, your breathing slows to long, deep breaths. Your body does it unconsciously. You can speed up the process of falling asleep by intentionally slowing your breaths to get your body ready to sleep.

Sleep Action #5: While laying in bed, take long, slow breaths. Count your breaths in your mind. Breathe in faster than you breathe out.

If meditation, gratitude, and breathing aren't enough to clear your mind, you probably have too much going on in there. Keep a pen and paper by your bed in case more ideas pop into your head while you're sleeping. Writing everything down releases your mind from the burden of trying to remember everything.

Sleep Action #6: Grab a pen and paper. At least ten minutes before you go to bed, write down everything that's on your mind. Don't edit. You don't have to make sense. Just write whatever pops into your head. What are you worried about? What do you need to do tomorrow? What do you need to remember? Do a complete brain dump until your mind is empty.

~

YOUR ENVIRONMENT

The most obvious, yet often overlooked, factor in sleep quality is your environment. Someone sleeping in a hot, noisy factory will not sleep as well as someone in a quiet, cozy room. You don't need someone to tell you that. Most likely your bedroom is not as extreme as a loud factory, so it won't be as obvious how you can improve it. What exactly are the ideal sleeping conditions?

Of course, it will vary from person to person, but for most people, a good sleeping environment is cool, dark, and free from distractions.

Sleep Action #7: At least at the beginning of the night when you are trying to fall asleep, keep the temperature at near 68°F if possible. You can raise the temperature later if you feel cold in the night.

Sleep Action #8: Make your room as dark as possible—pitch black being ideal—because there are studies that show even your skin can sense the presence of light.

Sleep Action #9: Remove all distractions including phones, television, and noise. Keep work out of the bedroom. Working in your bedroom creates a psychological connection between your bedroom and work stress.

Air quality is also an essential factor. If the air is too humid or too dry, it may affect your sleep. The ideal humidity for sleep is between 30% and 50%.

Sleep Action #10: Get a (de-)humidifier. Use a humidifier overnight if the humidity falls below 30%. Install a dehumidifier if it regularly goes over 50%. A hygrometer is an instrument that measures moisture in the air. They are inexpensive and work like a thermometer.

Sleep Action #11: Using sleep-inducing scents such as lavender, geranium, chamomile, or ylang-ylang can also help.

At night, avoid exposure to blue light. Blue light inhibits natural melatonin production. Managing your exposure to light will regulate your body's natural hormone production so you can fall asleep and wake easier.

Sleep Action #12: Avoid computer screens and fluorescent lighting at night because they give off blue light.

Many people, especially in urban environments, cannot control the noises coming from outside. If noise coming in from outside is bothersome, you can control the sounds in your bedroom.

Sleep Action #13: Play soothing music, nature sounds, or white noise while you sleep.

~

YOUR HEALTH

Your health can have a significant effect on your sleep. Diet and exercise play a huge role in how well you sleep. First, we'll discuss your diet.

It's best not to eat anything within a couple of hours of going to bed. Your body's digestion of the food may keep you up at night. Regulating your meal times can also control your hormone levels and sleep cycles. Ideally, you should eat a diet high in sleep nutrients such as selenium, vitamin C, trypto-phan, potassium, calcium, vitamin D, omega-3s, melatonin, vitamin B6, probiotics and prebiotics, and magnesium. The right foods to eat for high-quality sleep include green leafy vegetables, seeds like pumpkin and sesame, spirulina, brazil nuts, and organic, unprocessed foods. If you need to eat before bed, go for a high-fat, low-carb meal. Morning is the ideal time to have a big, nutritious meal.

Sleep Action #14: Avoid eating two hours before bedtime. If you're hungry before you sleep, eat a high-fat, low-carb snack.

People tend to underestimate how caffeine affects their sleep. The half-life of caffeine in most healthy adults is about 5-6 hours. That means if you consume 100mg of caffeine (the amount in a typical cup of coffee) at 4 PM, you might still have 50mg in your system at 10 PM. 25mg of caffeine would remain in your body at 4 AM. The fact is, taking caffeine at any time of the day can cause sleep problems. But if you're not ready to give up your coffee or tea habit, you can at least cut its impact by drinking it only before 2 PM. That would allow time for most of the caffeine to clear your system before you sleep.

· · ·

Sleep Action #15: Don't take caffeine after 2 PM.

If you have good sleep habits, you should be most energetic in the morning. Take advantage of the energy by doing exercise first thing when you wake up. If you have trouble motivating yourself, get an accountability partner to exercise with you every morning. Many people enjoy going out for a jog as soon as they get up. It has the added benefit of allowing you to get some morning sunlight as well. You should also incorporate some strength training into your regimen at least twice a week. Doing resistance exercises before bed can also help you fall asleep faster.

Sleep Action #16: Get some exercise soon after you wake up. Do some strength exercises before you go to bed.

～

SLEEP HACKS

In this section, you will find some unconventional things you can try for improving your sleep. These actions are either unintuitive or not suitable for long-term use.

Sleep Action #17: Try the Half Military Crawl. The most

straightforward sleep hack you can do is to adjust your position. You've been sleeping your whole life, so you know which position helps you sleep best. When you go to bed, arrange yourself into your best sleep position from the beginning. When in doubt, self-experimenter Timothy Ferriss recommends the Half Military Crawl position in his book The 4-Hour Body. In this position, you sleep on your stomach with one arm pointing towards your feet and the leg straight on that side. Bend your other arm and leg. This sleeping position works because it prevents you from moving in your sleep.

Sleep Action #18: Take a hot bath. Hot baths at bedtime may increase the release of melatonin to help you sleep. Take the bath an hour or two before going to bed.

Sleep Action #19: Take caffeine naps. People tend to get sleepy after lunch. The early afternoon is the ideal time for a caffeine nap. Drink a cup of strong coffee, then set an alarm for 20 minutes and close your eyes. You should be able to fall asleep for a few minutes and wake up to your alarm feeling invigorated. Be careful not to nap for more than 20 minutes. If you fall into deep sleep and are interrupted, you could feel worse upon waking.

. . .

Sleep Action #20: Smash your gut. CrossFit performance coach Kelly Starrett recommends rolling on your stomach with a medicine ball every day. In his book Tools of Titans, Timothy Ferriss remarks that doing this exercise also works as a sleep aid.

Sleep Action #21: Try polyphasic sleep. Breaking your sleep time into two or more chunks lets you spend less overall time sleeping. It helps you take advantage of the critical REM portions of sleep. In its most extreme form, polyphasic sleep involves taking six 20-minute naps spaced evenly throughout a 24-hour day—a total of two hours of sleep. A milder form of polyphasic sleep is taking 20-minute naps during the day as needed whenever you didn't get enough sleep at night. Find out more about polyphasic sleep online by searching your favorite search engine for "polyphasic sleep."

Sleep Action #22: Try the power of cold. Taking an ice bath before bed can help you fall into a deep slumber quickly. Dump 2-3 bags of ice into a tub half-full with water. Immerse your lower body for five minutes, then your upper torso for another five minutes. If ice baths are too extreme for you, taking a cold shower or walking outside in the cold before bed may have similar effects.

SUPPLEMENTS

Anything you eat can be considered a supplement, especially if taken outside of your regular meals. Bedtime snacks are no different. What you put in your body before you hit the sack can make a big difference in how well you sleep.

Sleep Action #23: Drink non-alcoholic beer. Hops used to make beer are thought to improve sleep. But, although alcohol can help you fall asleep faster, it can reduce the quality of your sleep. That means drinking non-alcoholic beer before bed may help you sleep better.

Sleep Action #24: Try the honey and apple cider vinegar tonic. Taking one or two tablespoons of honey at bedtime can improve your sleep. Your brain prioritizes the sugars from honey for use while you sleep. It results in a deeper, more restorative slumber. Apple cider vinegar helps digestion and breakdown of foods to release tryptophan. The combination of honey and apple cider vinegar is a favorite tonic for combating insomnia.

Sleep Action #25: Drink chamomile tea. Chamomile tea is often used to soothe the stomach and relax the muscles. Drink it before bed to fall asleep easier.

. . .

Sleep Action #26: Take probiotics. It can be hard to sleep when your stomach is hard at work digesting the food you ate before going to bed. It can be even harder to fall asleep when your stomach is having trouble digesting the food you ate. Probiotics are microorganisms that help your gut break down and digest the food you've eaten. Taking them can improve your health and reduce stomach and intestinal problems. Vary the brands that you use, so you gain exposure to many different types of microorganisms.

Sleep Action #27: Try pumpkin seed powder. Pumpkin seed powder is rich in the amino acid tryptophan, which helps your body produce melatonin and regulate your sleep.

Sleep Action #28: Take valerian root. Extracts of valerian root have sedative effects and can reduce anxiety.

Sleep Action #29: Take melatonin. Melatonin is a hormone that your body produces to regulate sleep cycles. Taking 1.5-3.0 milligrams of melatonin an hour before sleep may help. While taking melatonin is not addictive, taking it too often can inhibit your body's natural production of it.

~

TOOLS OF THE SLEEP MASTERS

Sleep Action #30: Get Flux (www.justgetflux.com). Blue light from your device screens can suppress your body's sleep hormones and prevent you from falling asleep at night. Flux is free software that automatically removes the blue light from your computer screen after the sun goes down, resulting in an orange tint.

Sleep Action #31: Wear a sleep mask. It's not always practical to remove all light from your room. In situations where you can't control the lighting, you can wear a sleep mask. You may also want to pair the sleep mask with earplugs, especially while traveling.

Sleep Action #32: Track your sleep. Tracking is vital to the development of any habit. The sleep habit is no different. For a more accurate measure of your sleep, try using a sleep tracker. Wristband tracking devices like FitBit can be used to track sleep. Search "sleep tracker" on Amazon to find more such devices. If you have a smartphone, you can download apps that track your sleep by detecting movement from your bed mattress (Try Sleep Cycle, www.sleepcycle.com). Track your sleep nightly, so you can see if you are improving.

. . .

Sleep Action #33: Get a noise machine. If you can't sleep in silence, you might as well choose the type of noise you sleep with. Get a noise machine to play white noise or soothing background sounds.

Sleep Action #34: Get blackout curtains. Most curtains are made from fabric that allows light to pass through. Blackout curtains are thicker and shut out all light from entering the room. They are essential if you need to sleep during the daytime unless you wear a sleep mask.

Sleep Action #35: Use artificial light cues. Many people have responsibilities that don't allow them to wake with the rising sun. If you have to wake up earlier than the sun, you can use artificial light to help you wake. Various companies make lights that create artificial sunlight. Search "phototherapy" on your favorite search engine or electronics retailer for more information.

Sleep Action #36: Get a ChiliPad. The ChiliPad is a mattress pad with a temperature control system that can warm or cool your bed with a thermostat.

. . .

Sleep Action #37: Try an Acupressure Mat. Acupressure mats lay on top of your mattress and have little soft spikes on them. You lay on top of them when you sleep, and the small spikes cause a slight discomfort that helps you to relax and fall asleep.

~

RESOURCES

Sleep Action #38: Learn more about sleep on the Web. The following are nonprofit websites dedicated to sleep research and education.

- The National Sleep Foundation (www. sleepfoundation.org)
- The Division of Sleep Medicine at Harvard Medical School (sleep.med.harvard.edu)
- Sleep Education (www.sleepeducation.org)

Sleep Action #39: Read more about sleep. Here are a few books that I recommend for learning more about sleep.

- *Sleep Smarter: 21 Essential Strategies to Sleep Your Way to a Better Body, Better Health, and Bigger Success,* by Shawn Stevenson

- *The Sleep Revolution: Transforming Your Life, One Night at a Time*, by Arianna Huffington
- *At Day's Close: Night in Times Past*, by A. Roger Ekirch
- *24/7: Late Capitalism and the Ends of Sleep*, by Jonathan Crary
- *4-Hour Body: An Uncommon Guide to Rapid Fat Loss, Incredible Sex and Becoming Superhuman*, by Timothy Ferriss
- *Tools of Titans: The Tactics, Routines, and Habits of Billionaires, Icons, and World-Class Performers*, by Timothy Ferriss

Sleep Action #40: Watch TED talks on sleep. If you're more of a visual learner, watching videos can be more helpful than reading books. *Talks to Inspire You to Go to Bed and Get a Good Night's Sleep* (www.ted.com/playlists/223/talks_to_inspire_you_to_go_to) is a curated playlist of TED talks that teach the importance of sleep.

Chapter Three

TIME MANAGEMENT

Question 1: How many things remain on your to-do list at the end of the day?

Your answer:

- More than 20: 0 points.
- 6-19: 1 point.
- Five or fewer: 2 points.

To-do lists tend to grow instead of shrink when you don't manage time well. Mine swelled to hundreds of tasks at one point. The ideal number of things to have on a to-do list is the amount of work you can do in one day. Usually, that's five or fewer to-do items.

Question 2: How are you doing on your most significant goal?

Your answer:

- I fell behind: 0 points.
- I'm stressed, but on pace: 1 point.
- It's under control, and on time or ahead: 2 points.

Most people are working on a big project. Whether it's a consulting project or a painting, you're probably trying to meet a deadline. How you keep pace to reach the deadline is also an indicator of your time management skills.

Question 3: How structured is your day?

Your answer:

- I do everything whenever I want: 0 points.

- Somewhat unstructured: 1 point.
- I do everything at scheduled times like clockwork: 2 points.

It's tough to manage time when you don't pay attention to it. An important aspect of time management is consistency. If you do tasks at the same time every day, you're more likely to complete them.

Add up all your points and see how you fared.

- 0-2 points: Read this chapter now.
- 3-4 points: Come back to this chapter later.
- 5-6 points: Skip this chapter, you're good.

~

THE IMPORTANCE OF TIME MANAGEMENT

Productivity is how much you get done in a day. It is a measure of the sheer volume of work you get done. You might have heard the saying, "quality over quantity," or vice versa. Productivity is like quantity, whereas effectiveness is like quality. Effectiveness is how meaningful the work is. One can be productive, but not effective. A productive painter might produce a hundred low-quality pieces of art in a month. If nobody buys them, he is ineffective. An unproductive painter can be effective if she produces a single painting in a year that sells for hundreds of thousands of dollars.

Time management is all about maximizing both productivity and effectiveness in the time you have. You want to be as productive **and** effective as possible. Choose the best action and do it quickly and efficiently. Everyone has the same twenty-four hours in a day. The most successful people are the ones who make the best use of each hour.

You can always make more money, but you can't make more time. If you want to live a fulfilled life, you must master time management skills. Ultimately, we don't know how long we have to live. That's why time management is so important. If you knew that you would die in your sleep tonight, would you regret doing what you're doing right now instead of something else? Make every hour of your time count towards something meaningful to you.

~

MORNING ROUTINE

Almost all successful people have a morning routine that energizes them for the rest of the day. Many of them use the first part of their day to get the bulk of their work done. Motivational coach and author Hal Elrod calls the first hour of his morning the "Miracle Morning." The point of the Miracle Morning is to do a few minutes of each of the essential things in your life. For Hal, it was meditation, affirmations, visualization, exercise, reading, and writing. You might choose different things to do for your Miracle Morning.

Time Management Action #1: Spend the first hour of your day in a "Miracle Morning" routine.

You might say, "I don't have an extra hour in the morning." Yes, you do. You're just spending that time sleeping or doing other things. The simple solution is to wake up an hour earlier. If doing so will cause you to get too little sleep (and getting enough sleep is very important), you might have to make time in other ways.

Here are some things you can try:

Time Management Action #2: Stop snoozing your alarm clock. Get up immediately with your alarm. Splash cold water on your face if you have to. But stop snoozing.

Time Management Action #3: Prepare for your morning at night. Don't waste time in the morning packing your lunch box or deciding what to wear. Prepare for the following day as much as you can before you go to sleep.

Time Management Action #4: If you eat breakfast, make it quick. You can still eat healthily. Have a piece of fruit, a bagel, microwave eggs, butter coffee, oatmeal, or whatever you can prepare in five minutes or less. You can always eat something more substantial if you have time after your morning hour.

Time Management Action #5: Take less time for morning hygiene activities. You may be able to shave a few minutes off of your current morning routine. Take a minute less time to shower. Spend a couple of minutes less time on the toilet. Don't stare at yourself in the mirror so long. It all adds up.

Time Management Action #6: Keep all electronics off as long as possible. Don't check email, texts, and social media first thing in the morning. That stuff can wait.

Time Management Action #7: Go to bed earlier. Each minute you go to bed earlier is an extra minute you have in the morning. You can even make it a gradual process where you try to sleep five minutes earlier each day.

. . .

When I was writing this book, I didn't get much done for the first couple months. Then I discovered the magic of doing the essential things first thing in the morning. It is 5:53 AM as I type this. Every morning I wake up at 5:00 AM and write for an hour before I do anything else. The world is quiet. I can focus on a single task. This habit alone ensures that I write 500-1,000 words a day.

Once you have that extra hour in the morning, you need to fill it up with invigorating activities. You want to start each day with a win. Starting the day with a win begins a domino effect that makes the rest of your day better. Ask yourself, "what is the single most important thing I have to do today?" Your most important thing is often your most difficult task or the one you've been putting off the longest. Be sure to incorporate your most important function into your morning routine. Make progress on your most important task during the first hour of your day. If you can do that, your day will be productive no matter what you do with the rest of the day.

Time Management Action #8: Start the most important task during the first hour of your day.

∼

SCHEDULING YOUR DAY

What gets scheduled gets done.

Never start your day unplanned. In fact, you should even begin planning your day the night before. As much as possible, you want to hit the ground running from the moment you open your eyes in the morning. So how do you go about planning your day?

There is a well-known story of a professor who fills a jar with rocks and asks his students if the jar is full. When they confirm that the jar is full, he proves them wrong by pouring a bag of sand into the jar. It wouldn't have worked the other way around. If the professor had poured the sand into the jar first, the rocks wouldn't have fit. Schedule the big things first and fit the smaller tasks around them.

How do you know what the "big things" are? The first question to ask yourself is, "what do I do?" I'm a writer, so my big thing is writing. If you're a teacher, your big thing is teaching. If you're a truck driver, your big thing is driving trucks. But you probably want to go more detailed than that. So now we apply the 80/20 rule. That is, "what 20% of tasks produce 80% of the results?" As a writer, I can tell you that writing is one of the "20% of tasks," while posting on Facebook is not. A third question you can ask is, "what is the one thing that I can do that will make today a success?" Once you've figured out what your big things are, schedule them on a calendar. It's not real unless it's on your calendar.

. . .

Time Management Action #9: Determine your most important tasks.

When you schedule your tasks, batch the similar ones together. Opt for larger blocks of time whenever possible. For example, if you check your email three times a day, why not explore checking it twice a day, or even once a day? The more segmented your day is, the more inefficient it becomes.

Time Management Action #10: Batch similar tasks together and schedule them on your calendar.

Another consideration is Parkinson's Law. Your work expands to fill the time you allot it. If you give yourself a week to write a document, it will take the entire week. But if you give yourself two days to do it, you will finish it in two days. Don't set impossible deadlines, but your deadlines should be close enough to keep you on your toes.

Time Management Action #11: For the most important tasks, decide how much time you need to complete them. Give yourself about 10% less time to do each task.

. . .

Consider your working rhythm and energy levels. Each person works differently. Some people are night owls while others work best in the morning. Keep in mind that your most important tasks probably require the most energy and willpower to complete. Schedule the most important tasks for times when you work best.

Time Management Action #12: Determine your most productive work times. Schedule your most critical tasks for those times.

Remember the story of the rocks and sand going into the jar? Once you've filled your schedule with the big tasks, identify the small tasks that you can do to fill in the small spaces of time between the big tasks. Maybe you can check email while standing in line to get your lunch. Or do some meditation while sitting on the subway to work. You might be able to make a few phone calls between tasks in the afternoon.

Time Management Action #13: Do all the small tasks in the time gaps between big tasks.

Finally, realize that it's okay to say "no." You can't do everything. Delegate some tasks to others. While it's good to say "yes" to most opportunities early in your career, you should say "no" more often as you progress.

~

PHYSICAL

You need to stay in good health if you want to stay productive. You won't get a lot of work done if you're in the hospital and feeling bad. Eating well and staying fit will also increase your energy levels so you can maintain productive work.

Time Management Action #14: Drink water. Dehydration can make you feel lethargic and weak. Make sure you drink plenty of water throughout the day. Eight glasses a day is the commonly given guideline. Schedule your water drinking if you have to.

Time Management Action #15: Take breaks. Take a break every half hour or hour. If you sit to work, make sure you get up and walk around. Unless you're "in the zone," your productivity will diminish as you work. Taking a break is an excellent way to refresh yourself and reset your productivity.

. . .

Time Management Action #16: Exercise. Many successful people attribute their ability to get a lot of work done to their exercise routine. It's counterintuitive, but exercising gives you more energy and increases creativity. Do it as early as possible in the day for maximum effect.

Time Management Action #17: Get enough sleep. It's better to sleep eight hours and do four hours of focused energetic work than to sleep four hours and do eight hours of work while you're sleepy. You'll get more done in the four hours of rested work than in the eight hours of tired work. The quality of the work you do while well-rested will be much better than work you do while sleepy.

Time Management Action #18: Meditate. Meditating is like hitting the "reset" button on your brain. You empty your thoughts and start fresh. Breathe, and be productive again.

Time Management Action #19: Eat. You can't work if half your brain is thinking about food. Eat frequent, small meals. Healthy foods will give you better energy. Some suggestions include greens, eggs, salmon, berries, eggplant, chocolate, green tea, and garlic. Avoid eating sugar and junk food. Also avoid eating too little, as that will decrease your energy levels.

~

DOING THE WORK

The most important part of time management is taking time to *actually do useful work*. That means doing your work quickly and efficiently while keeping distractions at bay.

Having the right tools for the job is essential. As Abraham Lincoln alluded to when he said "Give me six hours to chop down a tree and I will spend the first four sharpening the ax," you can probably chop down a tree easily in two hours if you have a sharp ax. But if you're using a dull ax, it might well be impossible.

What tools do you need for your task? If you're not sure, look at what the professionals use. Apply the 80/20 Rule to find the 20% of tools that get 80% of the job done. Then organize your work area so that it's free from distractions and you have plenty of space to work.

Time Management Action #20: Decide what tools you need to do your job, then procure them before starting work.

As you work, focus on one task at a time. Multitasking does not work for the vast majority of people. Most people can stay focused for somewhere between 20 and 50 minutes. Experiment with work "sprints" lasting between 20 and 50 minutes to see what works best for you. A sprint is a period of focused work. After you complete a work sprint, take a break of at least five minutes before starting work again.

Time Management Action #21: Ditch the multitasking. Do one task at a time in focused sprints.

~

HACKS

Business books love to toss around productivity hacks that can help you manage your time. Many of them are rehashed versions of old methods, but with catchy new names. A few of them have stood the test of time, though. Here are a few that have worked for me.

Time Management Action #22: Use the Pomodoro Method. Developed by Francesco Cirillo in the 1980s, this technique involves using a timer to manage work sprints. Cirillo named it after the tomato-shaped Pomodoro kitchen timer. The standard method is to do focused work for 25 minutes, then take a five-minute break. After four sessions of concentrated work, take a longer, 30-minute break. Many apps use the technique. Search for "Pomodoro timer" on a search engine

or your phone's app store. The official website is at www.
pomodorotechnique.com.

Time Management Action #23: Try Getting Things Done
(or GTD). It is a method of doing work described in a book
by the same name, by David Allen. It involves collecting
tasks, then processing, organizing, planning, and doing them.
One helpful hack in GTD is the Two Minute Rule. Whenever
you're looking at your to-do list, if you see something that
takes less than two minutes to do, do it immediately. Read
more about GTD at the official website (www.
gettingthingsdone.com).

Time Management Action #24: Don't Break the Chain. It
was advice that comedian Jerry Seinfeld once gave to software developer Brad Isaac when he was performing stand-up
at open-mic nights. It makes a game out of your work. Identify your most important daily task. For Seinfeld, it was
writing jokes. Get a calendar and put it in your work area.
Each day you do your essential daily task, put a big red "X"
on today's date on the calendar. In Seinfeld's case, on each
day he wrote a joke, he would put an "X" on the day. See how
many days in a row you can do it. Don't break the chain, or
you'll have to start over.

. . .

Time Management Action #25: Go on a media diet. Many people waste much of their productive day browsing media. Whether it's social media, entertainment, or news, you can afford to cut much of it out of your life. Try a "media detox" by avoiding consuming media for one week. See how it affects your productivity.

Time Management Action #26: Speed up your typing. If you spend most of your time working on your computer, it helps to learn touch typing. Touch typists type at twice the speed of "hunt and peck" typists. If your job requires a lot of typing, learning touch typing can translate into hours of saved time. One of the most popular ways to learn touch typing is the Mavis Beacon Teaches Typing line of software products. You can find them at www.mavisbeacon.com.

Time Management Action #27: Learn the shortcuts. Another way to speed up your computer usage is by using keyboard shortcuts. Learn the keyboard shortcuts for each of your most-used software applications. You can find the keyboard shortcuts for any software application by browsing through the application's menus. The shortcuts are typically noted on the righthand side of the menu options. Another way to find the keyboard shortcuts is to search the application's help documentation for "keyboard shortcuts."

~

SUPPLEMENTS

There are supplements out there that can help you increase productivity. To do so, you should look for the supplements that improve your focus and energy. As with all supplements, you should consult your doctor before taking any of them.

Time Management Action #28: Drink caffeinated beverages. Caffeine is the most popular choice for productivity. It usually comes in the form of coffee or tea. Soda and chocolate also contain caffeine. Your body can get desensitized from overuse, so it's best to avoid taking caffeine on a daily basis. Use it as a secret weapon for those times when you need to boost your awareness and energy levels temporarily.

Time Management Action #29: Take Ginkgo biloba for concentration. Extracts of the Ginkgo biloba leaf are commonly sold as cognitive enhancers. As with many herbal supplements, there is little scientific proof to back the claims. However, it may be worth a try.

Time Management Action #30: Take eleuthero. Also known as Siberian ginseng, eleuthero is a small, woody shrub with a history of use in traditional Chinese medicine. In alternative medicine, it is touted as a mental performance booster.

Time Management Action #31: Try ginseng. Ginseng has been used for centuries as a traditional medicine. Though modern research is inconclusive about its effects, some research shows possible memory and energy enhancing effects.

Time Management Action #32: Use rosemary. Rosemary is a common herb that contains several phytochemicals that may have beneficial health effects. One possible effect of rosemary is in improving memory.

~

TOOLS

There is no shortage of productivity tools out there. Most of them these days come in the form of smartphone apps.

Years ago, before the internet and smartphones, people developed physical productivity techniques. Pencil and paper was king. People stored information in notebooks, 3-ring binders, and filing cabinets.

. . .

Time Management Action #33: Use an all-in-one office suite. Microsoft Office and Google G Suite provide word processors, spreadsheets, calendars, e-mail, and many other digital office features to help you run your business. They mimic the functions of physical offices. Having a single suite of software for all office functions keeps your user interfaces consistent and saves you time.

Time Management Action #34: Have an idea capture system. You can go old-school and buy notebooks to take notes. A three-ring binder is a good place to keep project notes and workflows. If you want to go digital, Evernote (www.evernote.com) is the most popular choice. Google Keep (keep.google.com) is a free alternative that I currently use. When you have an idea capture system, you don't need to waste brainpower mulling new ideas in your head before your current project is finished.

Time Management Action #35: Use a task manager. *Things* (https://culturedcode.com/things/) stores your goals and tasks in one place. Keep your to-do lists in the app and schedule reminders. Manage projects and prioritize tasks. The app helps you always to know what to do next.

Time Management Action #36: Use calendar apps. When

choosing a calendar app to use, make sure it stores data in the cloud, and you can access it from all your devices. Every major operating system has a native cloud calendar app. Microsoft has Outlook Calendar (calendar.live.com). Apple has iCloud Calendar (calendar.icloud.com). Google has Google Calendar (calendar.google.com).

Time Management Action #37: Automate. IFTTT (www.ifttt.com) stands for "IF This Then That." You can use it to create chains of commands that get triggered by websites and apps. It grabs data from other apps and uses it to make decisions and automate tasks. With it, you can save liked tweets on Twitter to a Google spreadsheet. You can get an email whenever the President signs a bill into law. Add tomorrow's weather report to your calendar every day at 6 PM. And thousands more. The possibilities are endless.

Time Management Action #38: Track your time usage with an app. Performance coach Jairek Robbins uses ATracker (www.wonderapps.se/atracker) to help people track their time. Monitoring time creates a level of awareness that allows you to avoid time-wasting activities and do more productive tasks.

Time Management Action #39: Save time typing. TextExpander (www.textexpander.com) saves time by substituting typed text codes with preset blocks of text. For example, you might set it so that every time you type "_address", it enters your full address instead.

~

RESOURCES

Time Management Action #40: Listen to time management podcasts. You can find podcasts dedicated to productivity on your favorite podcast app. Here are a few good ones:

- Beyond the To Do List, with Erik Fisher.
- The Productivity Show, by Asian Efficiency.
- The Productivityist Podcast, with Mike Vardy
- The Productivity Podcast, with Paul Minors

Time Management Action #41: Read productivity blogs to get the most up-to-date tips for time management.

- Lifehacker (www.lifehacker.com).
- Lifehack (www.lifehack.org).
- Time Management Ninja (www.timemanagementninja.com)
- Brian Tracy (www.briantracy.com)

Time Management Action #42: Watch TED talks on time management.

- David Grady: How to save the world (or at least yourself) from bad meetings (www.youtube.com/watch?v=F6Qo8IDsVNg)
- Paolo Cardini: Forget multitasking, try monotasking (www.youtube.com/watch?v=0YNeyBANrTI)
- David Pogue: 10 top time-saving tech tips (www.youtube.com/watch?v=QoT0-2vu9m4)
- Laura Vanderkam: How to gain control of your free time (www.ted.com/talks/laura_vanderkam_how_to_gain_control_of_your_free_time)

Time Management Action #43: Read books on time management.

- *The 4-Hour Workweek: Escape 9-5, Live Anywhere, and Join the New Rich*, by Timothy Ferriss.
- *Getting Things Done: The Art of Stress-Free Productivity*, by David Allen.
- *The Productivity Project: Accomplishing More by*

Managing Your Time, Attention, and Energy, by Chris Bailey

- *15 Secrets Successful People Know About Time Management: The Productivity Habits of 7 Billionaires, 13 Olympic Athletes, 29 Straight-A Students, and 239 Entrepreneurs,* by Kevin Kruse

Chapter Four

CAREER

How do you know if you're where you want to be in your career? Not everyone wants to be an entrepreneur. While working for yourself has its benefits, many people don't want to call all the shots. In many ways, it's easier to let other people find clients and decide what work needs to be done. If you're a career person, how do you know you're moving in the right direction?

Question 1: Do you look forward to each day at your job?

Your answer:

- I dread going to work: 0 points.

- I like my job, but feel that something is missing: 1 point.
- I love my job: 2 points.

Question 2: Are you paid enough?

Your answer:

- No: 0 points.
- Yes, but not enough to save a lot of money: 1 point.
- Yes: 2 points.

Question 3: Where do you want to be in ten years? Will your current career path take you there?

Your answer:

- No: 0 points.
- Yes, but I won't reach my ten-year goal in ten years on my current path: 1 point.
- Yes: 2 points.

If you're planning on spending your next ten, twenty, or forty years working a career, you better enjoy it. Life is too short to spend it dreading each day of your job. Everyone has talents that they can contribute to society through hard work. If you're not in the right career, work towards switching to one that's better suited to you. If you are in the right job, you need to make sure you're on a path that can keep you happy in the long term.

Add up all your points and see how you fared.

- 0-2 points: Read this chapter now.
- 3-4 points: Come back to this chapter later.
- 5-6 points: Skip this chapter, you're good.

IMPORTANCE OF CAREER

A career is more than just your job. *The Oxford English Dictionary* defines it as your "course or progress through life." It is the sum of all your learning, work, and achievements.

The career you choose is one of the most important decisions of your life. Before you can choose the perfect career, you have to find meaning in your life. But paradoxically, you often will not find your life's calling until you have walked down a few different paths.

The only way to find meaning and a satisfying career is by taking action. I can't tell you what the purpose of your life is because it is highly personal. But I can tell you that it's not idleness.

How do you know when you've found the right career for you? It's when you can't wait to get back to work. It's when you wake up in the morning energized because you're excited to see what's in store for you that day. If you haven't reached that point yet, move on. You need to build up to your dream career. Take one step at a time. As long as you're stepping in the right direction, you're making progress. Every step in your career path will come with its challenges. No step will be easy. Just keep moving.

Continue until you've found the career that matches your calling. Then keep moving.

When choosing a job, there are many factors you should consider. List each position you are considering and write down each of the factors. There are three types of factors you should consider: objective, subjective, and interpersonal. Objective factors include salary, benefits, location, and career advancement opportunities. Subjective factors include the social status of the job, the reputation of the organization, and your enthusiasm for the job. Interpersonal factors include professionalism of the people in the organization and how well you get along with your leaders and coworkers.

. . .

Career Action #1: If you are unsure of the career path to pursue, try taking some career assessment tests. Some tests you can take include the Strong Interest Inventory, the Myers-Briggs Type Indicator, Careerscope, and Traitify.

Generations ago, careers were more straightforward. You went to the best schools you could. Then, using your school transcripts, you went to work for the most respected company you could get hired into. Once you got into a company, you would do everything your bosses told you to do. That would ensure you kept moving up in your organization until you retired at age 65. That was the definition of "career" back then.

Now things are more complicated. The Internet flattened the playing field. There is no longer one clear path that you should take. Fewer people know their destination. As a result, many people wander between different jobs and different careers, not knowing what their ultimate goal is. Instead of competing with ten neighbors for five local jobs, now you're competing with a billion other people for half a billion jobs.

To have a successful career today, you need to sharpen your toolset. It's no longer okay to blindly follow a path that others have chosen for you.

ENTHUSIASM FOR WORK AND LIFE

Mindset is everything. Take two people with opposing outlooks on life and put them in the same job. The person with the positive attitude will learn and thrive. The negative person will act hostile towards the job. Negative people close their minds and refuse to grow. The simplest strategy for climbing the career ladder is to stay positive no matter what negativity surrounds you. People will notice your positivity. They will enjoy working with you. And, as a result, they will want to keep you around.

Will Bowen, the author of *A Complaint Free World*, claims that 78% of workers in the United States waste an average of 4.5 hours a week listening to coworkers complain. What can you do with an extra 4.5 hours a week? People complain about problems to remove themselves from responsibility. Complaining doesn't solve any problems. It's just a round-about way of asking others to solve them for you. Bowen advocates wearing a bracelet. Whenever you catch yourself complaining, switch the bracelet to the other hand. Over time, you will gain an awareness of complaining. You will complain less and take more responsibility.

Career Action #2: Wear a "no complaints" bracelet. You can learn more or order bracelets at Will Bowen's website (www. willbowen.com).

. . .

The best people at a company are the people who know the most about it. If you want to advance at your job, you'd best learn its history. Read about your company. Talk to people about it. Buy and use your company's products if it's practical. Learn about your job and become your company's ultimate fanboy or fangirl. Live and breathe it. People will notice. When it comes time to promote someone, they will think of you. Because you are the personification of your company. What better person is there to lead it?

Career Action #3: Learn everything you can about your job and your company.

~

NETWORKING

The lifeblood of any company is its people. A company without people is just a system. A system is stagnant and rigid. As soon as something changes in the world, the system breaks. It takes people to keep a company running.

If you want to succeed in an organization, you need to get to know the people within it. After all, it will be people who promote you, not some faceless system protocol. Be active within your organization. Attend company events. Go to conferences. Take every opportunity to spend time with your coworkers and bosses. The relationships you build will be invaluable to the future of your career. According to a 2016 survey (www.linkedin.com/pulse/new-survey-reveals-85-all-jobs-filled-via-networking-lou-adler), 85% of jobs are filled through networking.

The key to successful networking is interpersonal skills. It's a nebulous term that many companies list as a requirement in their job descriptions. What does it mean? A person with strong interpersonal skills works well with others and communicates well.

Career Action #4: Develop your interpersonal skills. Every time you interact with someone, practice the following skills:

- Try to stay positive and smile as much as you can when interacting with others.
- Listen carefully to others when they talk. Don't speak until others are finished. Notice their choice of words and inflections.
- Pay attention to nonverbal cues such as eye contact, gestures, and the direction their feet are pointing.
- Try to understand why others feel the way they do. Think about their incentives and motives.
- Recognize the achievements of others and thank them for their work. Gratitude goes a long way towards building rapport.
- Don't assume or presume things. Confirm

everything in your communication. Don't gossip. Consider every idea. Settle disputes.

- Use humor as your secret weapon for breaking communication barriers.

American author and motivational speaker Jim Rohn famously said, "You are the average of the five people you spend the most time with." Take special care when you choose the people you spend time with. Spend more time with people you respect and admire. Learn everything you can from them.

Career Action #5: Who are the five people you admire most? Try to spend time with them as much as possible. If you don't know them personally, follow their work closely. Visit their websites, listen to their podcasts, and read their books. Make your chosen five your mentors.

~

MASTER YOUR CRAFT

The idea of a career is that you spend your working years progressing towards some ultimate goal. The goal might be a financial target, a particular lifestyle, or a specific position within the company. To reach the goal, you must achieve several milestones. It involves solving problems and constant learning and improvement.

To be successful in a career, you need to master your craft. Learn as much as you can and apply what you learned in your job. If you stop learning, you will likely stagnate in your career.

Career Action #6: Spend an hour to write down your long-term goals. Here are a few questions to get you thinking:

- You just had a billion dollars wired into your bank account. What will you do this week? What will your life look like five years from now?
- You were just hit by a bus and killed instantly. What will people say about you at your funeral? Is there anything you wish you had done with your life? What's holding you back from doing it today?
- What's on your bucket list? What do you want to do before you "kick the bucket" and die? What is the first step towards doing each item on your list? What can you do today to get closer to realizing your dreams?

Once you know what your long-term goals are, make a plan

for getting there. What skills do you need to learn? What milestones do you need to reach? I find it helpful to set learning goals and milestones each year. Set an ambitious yearlong goal for career growth today. Work towards it a little each day.

~

SIDE HUSTLE

The average millionaire has seven streams of income. Most people only think about one stream of income: their day job. Your day job will pay your bills. However, it won't make you wealthy. If you want to go beyond your salary, you will need a side hustle. A side hustle is something you do outside of your day job to make money that supplements your salary. Doing this allows you to keep your regular career while also creating more streams of income.

To create side hustles and multiple streams of income, you need to develop an entrepreneurial mentality. Get in the habit of always keeping your eyes open to opportunities for making money. It takes practice, but once you get the hang of it, you will begin to see more and more opportunities.

Career Action #7: Make a habit of always being on the lookout for opportunities. Here are a few types of opportuni-ties to keep an eye out for:

- Trends: You see something on the market that has great potential, but not everybody knows about it yet. You can find a way to invest in the trend to profit from it.
- Arbitrage: You see a product on the market and that you can buy for a low price and resell for a high price.
- Pain points: there is a problem or frustration, and no product on the market fixes it. You can come up with a solution to the pain point and sell it.
- Repackaging: You see a product on the market that is not marketed well. You can repackage and rebrand it to sell with better marketing techniques.
- Unpacking: if there is a product available only in large quantities, you can buy it and resell smaller portions of it.

~

HACKS

Almost by definition, careers are long-term events. While I don't suggest cutting corners at the expense of integrity, there are some hacks you can use to speed up your career.

Career Action #8: Pivot. Every year or so, devote a few hours to examining where you are in your career and whether it aligns with your goals. Time is too precious to waste. If something is not advancing your career, ask yourself how you will change the way you're doing things. Make a big career goal for the year. Break it up into smaller monthly milestones. Break those monthly milestones down further into daily goals. Make progress towards your big goal every day. Be relentless.

Career Action #9: Get organized. Clean your desk and work area. Remove anything you don't need for completing your job and put it out of sight. Organize your work materials for greatest efficiency. If you need to call someone every fifteen minutes, it doesn't make sense to keep your phone across the room from your desk. Make work as effortless as possible.

Career Action #10: Buy new office supplies. Sometimes having brand new supplies can get you excited enough to start the work you've been putting off.

Career Action #11: Get to work early. Arriving at work early every day will build your reputation as someone who is always on top of things. It also creates the perception that you work harder than other employees. Another advantage to arriving to work early is that there are often fewer distractions so you can get more work done.

. . .

Career Action #12: Look the part. Dress and act like the position you want to be. If you're going to become CEO of your company someday, you better start dressing like the CEO now. People don't magically change the way they dress as they move up the corporate ladder. If the CEO wears a suit to work every day, you can bet she wore a suit to work every day even as an entry-level worker. At the very least, try dressing a step classier than your coworkers. It doesn't stop at clothing either. You also need to act like the position you want. Develop good communication skills. Have proper posture. Act with confidence. Act successful.

Career Action #13: Make your boss look good. Your boss can make or break your future at your company. If you make your boss look bad, they are likely to break your future. But if you make them look good, they will make it. Don't worry about taking credit for yourself. Just worry about making your boss happy. Their success will trickle down to you. Always over-deliver.

Career Action #14: Ask for a promotion. Most of the time, it doesn't hurt to ask. Don't wait for your boss to promote you. It is in your boss' best interest to keep you at a lower level for as long as possible. Once you've built a reputation for over-delivering, go ahead and ask for a promotion. You don't get what you don't ask for.

~

SUPPLEMENTS

The best supplements for your career are the ones that increase your overall health, cognition, and focus. Your career represents your entire working life, which will likely span fifty or more years. Your focus should be long-term.

Because career and time management are closely linked, the supplements listed in the chapter on time management will also help you at your job. Most of them are short-term solutions. To avoid repeating information, this section will focus on supplements that may increase your longevity. If you want to have a successful career, you need to stay healthy throughout your working life. You want to live a long, productive life. Part of that is staying healthy as long as possible.

Career Action #15: Take vitamin D. Most people in modern society don't get enough vitamin D. Your body produces vitamin D when it's exposed to sunlight. Most people these days spend most of their time indoors. When they do go outdoors, they cover up with clothing, sunglasses, and sunblock. If this sounds like you, you're probably also deficient in vitamin D. Most people will do well with 1,000 IU of vitamin D3 supplements each day. To be sure, you should get your blood tested.

Career Action #16: Take fish oil. Your brain tissue is composed mostly of omega-3 fatty acids. Taking an omega-3 supplement like fish oil can improve your brain health. But taking omega-3 fatty acids is not enough. You also need to reduce the amount of omega-6 fatty acids. Omega-6 fatty acids are the "bad" oils that make up most of the oils on store shelves. What matters is not the amount of fatty acids you consume, but the ratio of omega-6 to omega-3. Try your best to decrease your omega-6 while increasing your omega-3.

Career Action #17: Take resveratrol. Resveratrol has been found to support a healthy heart. You can get it from red grape skins (and red wine), blueberries, and raspberries, among others.

Career Action #18: Get the right minerals. Certain minerals might increase your lifespan. Zinc helps maintain higher testosterone levels and supports your immune system. Magnesium aids a wide range of functions in your body from repairing cells to maintaining a healthy heart rhythm.

Chromium is critical to the production of insulin in your body, which helps regulate your weight.

Career Action #19: Take curcumin. Turmeric is a mild yellow spice that has been used in Asian cuisine and traditional medicine for generations. It contains curcumin, which is thought to have potent anti-inflammatory and antioxidant properties.

Career Action #20: Take carnitine. L-Carnitine is an amino acid found in red meats. It promotes fat burning and provides cardiovascular support, giving you more energy and endurance.

Career Action #21: Take alpha lipoic acid (ALA). Your body naturally creates ALA to use in metabolic functions. It is believed to help your body use insulin to break down glucose and reduce nerve damage caused by diabetes.

Career Action #22: Take CoQ_{10}. Coenzyme Q_{10} is another natural compound found in your body. It functions as an antioxidant and helps your cells produce energy.

~

TOOLS

It is difficult to create a list of purely "career" tools without overlapping with time management and personal finances. Career is such a broad topic that without a doubt I will miss some of the more niche and smaller tools in this list. So I will list here tools focused on learning, job searching, and management.

Career Action #23: Always be learning. If you don't have time to read business books, you can take advantage of a book abstract service like getAbstract (www.getabstract.com) or Blinkist (www.blinkist.com). These services create summaries of books with only the main points.

Career Action #24: Use networking tools. A strong professional network is the single greatest tool you can have to advance in your career. LinkedIn (www.linkedin.com) is a social media site for professionals. You can also boost your career on other social media sites like Facebook (www.facebook.com) and Twitter (www.twitter.com). Once you're on social media, join relevant groups or connect with other professionals in your field. JobHero (www.jobhero.com) helps you organize and follow up with your business contacts. MeetUp (www.meetup.com) helps you find meetings with other people in your career niche.

. . .

Career Action #25: Create your personal brand. Employers often search the web for prospective or current employees. Sites like BrandYourself (www.brandyourself.com) and Trackur (www.trackur.com) help you manage your online identity so you can present yourself to employers in the best possible light. Google Alerts (www.google.com/alerts) lets you set up notifications that will email you whenever new information about you is posted online. If you are tech-savvy, you can also register a domain name and create an official personal website. A personal website is a great place to show off your work portfolio.

Career Action #26: Do company research. Glassdoor (www.glassdoor.com) and Career Bliss (www.careerbliss.com) provide tools for researching companies. The information is useful when finding companies and for preparing for interviews. FairyGodboss (www.fairygodboss.com) lets women rate their employers and discuss issues that matter to them. Salary.com (www.salary.com) and PayScale.com (www.payscale.com) provide information on how much you can expect to make at different locations, companies, and career fields. ZoomInfo (www.zoominfo.com) provides information about businesses and professionals.

. . .

Career Action #27: Prepare for your interviews. Big Interview (www.biginterview.com) and Phone Interview Pro (www.phoneinterviewpro.com) are two tools that can help you in your interviews. You can also take part in mock interviews to polish your interviewing skills and spot mistakes, so you don't make them in real interviews.

Career Action #28: Use resume tools. Your resume is often the first impression you make to a company recruiter. It is the first test for whether an employer should even consider hiring you. The resume templates in Microsoft Word or Google Docs provide a good starting point for making an attractive resume. There are also resume builder apps like ineedaresu.me (www.ineedaresu.me), EnhanCV (www.enhancv.com), Sumry (www.sumry.me), CV Maker (www.cvmkr.com), or Creddle (www.creddle.io).

∿

RESOURCES

Almost every adult on Earth works in some way. Every working adult can benefit from career advice, so you can imagine how much career advice is available on the internet. I've compiled some of the most prominent, most popular career resources I could find.

· · ·

Career Action #29: Read career blogs.

- Penelope Trunk (www.penelopetrunk.com).
- Ask a Manager (www.askamanager.org).
- The Daily Muse (www.themuse.com/advice).

Career Action #30: Visit career websites.

- Careers.org (www.careers.org).
- CareerBuilder (www.careerbuilder.com).
- Monster.com (www.monster.com).
- Career Onestop (www.careeronestop.org).

Career Action #31: Take a self-assessment test. Ten excellent free career self-assessment tools on the Internet, by Catherine Conlan (www.monster.com/career-advice/article/best-free-career-assessment-tools). It has a listing of free and pay personality tests.

Career Action #32: Here are a few books that will give you valuable career advice:

- *The 7 Habits of Highly Effective People: Powerful Lessons in Personal Change,* by Stephen R. Covey.
- *What Color Is Your Parachute? 2017: A Practical Manual for Job-Hunters and Career-Changers,* by Richard N. Bolles.
- *How To Win Friends and Influence People,* by Dale Carnegie.
- *Unlimited Power: The New Science Of Personal Achievement,* by Tony Robbins.
- *Lean In: Women, Work, and the Will to Lead,* by Sheryl Sandberg.

Career Action #33: Listen to career podcasts during your commute.

- The Happen to Your Career Podcast (www. happentoyourcareer.com/podcast-2).
- Manager Tools Podcast (www.manager-tools.com/podcasts).
- The School of Greatness Podcast (https:// lewishowes.com/blog/).

Chapter Five

DIET

When most people think of the word "diet," they think of eating (or starving) to lose weight. Diet has a much broader meaning. Your diet is the sum of your eating habits. It's what you regularly put into your body for sustenance.

There is no easy way to measure how good or how bad your diet is. It depends on your health goals and what facts about health you believe to be true. A vegan might believe a Paleo diet to be unhealthy. A powerlifter might believe a vegan diet to be unsuitable to her goals. A marathon runner might criticize a powerlifter's diet. There is no correct diet for everyone. As a result, the questions in this quiz are subjective. Take a look at your eating habits and answer honestly.

· · ·

Question 1: How much thought goes into each meal you eat?

Your Answer:

- I eat whatever I want whenever I want: 0 points.
- I try to eat healthy when I can: 1 point.
- I meticulously plan every meal for optimum health: 2 points.

Question 2: How healthy do you think you eat?

Your Answer:

- I'm a junk food addict: 0 points.
- I eat a "normal" diet: 1 point.
- I always eat healthy: 2 points.

Question 3: How healthy does your doctor think you are?

Your Answer:

- My doctor has given me directives for what I should and should not eat: 0 points.
- There are areas of concern that a change of diet can fix (high cholesterol, obesity, etc.): 1 point.
- My doctor says I'm healthy: 2 points.

Add up all your points and see how you fared:

0-2 points: read this chapter now.

3-4 points: come back to this chapter later.

5-6 points: skip this chapter, you're good.

～

THE IMPORTANCE OF DIET

Sometimes the old cliches are old and overused because they are timeless truths. "You are what you eat" is one such truth. Think of your body as a system that has inputs and outputs. Every moment, you output from your body. Dead skin. Sweat. Heat. And that's not even mentioning the obvious outputs from your body. Since you cannot create or destroy matter, as per the laws of physics, you must replenish what you lose. Everything you eat or drink becomes new cells in your body or gets purged. In that sense, "you are what you eat" is quite literal.

I'm not here to tell you what you can or can't eat. Each

person has a unique body composition, situation, and goals. An ideal diet for one person can kill another person. Instead, I want to give you a list of ideas to consider when examining the foods you eat. I am not a doctor. If you see an idea you want to try, please discuss it with your doctor before starting.

One more note. Do you ever wonder why there are so many diet books and programs? I've tried at least a dozen different diets. They all work if you follow the instructions to the letter. But most people don't. They bounce around between various weight-loss plans and quit whenever one gets too inconvenient. Changing habits is hard. It's especially hard in a world where decadent pleasure foods are abundant. But there is a solution. You need an exit plan.

Whenever you make a change to your diet, think of it as a short-term change. Give yourself 30 days to try it. If after 30 days it doesn't work out, you have permission to quit. It doesn't even have to be as long as 30 days. Are you thinking of going vegan? Try it for one week. Or even one day. The goal is not all or nothing. The goal is to take action. Eating healthier for one day is better than taking the stagnant path of doing nothing.

Diet Action #1: Make a change to your diet for a week. If you get the results you're looking for, keep going. If it doesn't work out, it's okay to quit after the week.

~

NATURE'S WAY

Nature has a reason for everything. Be skeptical of anything that doesn't exist in nature. You don't have to shun technology, just be skeptical and weigh the pros and cons. When in doubt, eat whole foods and avoid processed foods. Human beings have been eating natural whole foods for thousands of years. We know for a fact that we can thrive eating foods as they exist in nature. But with processed foods, we tread into unknown territory.

At one extreme is fast food. Fast food is about making money. Fast food companies hire scientists and marketers to formulate the food that you crave. The scientists find cheaper ways of producing enticing foods. The marketers find ways to make you want to buy it. Your health is not their concern (unless showing concern will make them more money).

At the other extreme is the "Paleo" ideology. Paleo stands for the Paleolithic diet, as in, the diet people ate in the Stone Age. The so-called cavemen did not have the means to process foods like we do today. The Paleo diet represents the ultimate natural whole foods diet for humans. Skeptics like to point out that early humans did not live long. Also, there is much we don't know about how people lived 50,000 years ago.

It might be best for us to find a healthy middle ground somewhere between fast food and Paleo. For me, that means going Paleo when in doubt, but staying informed about new technology. Early humans did not refrigerate their foods or vary their diets. But I am thankful for refrigeration and modern transportation of food. Modern humans like to sweeten and process their foods. But science has also shown that sugar and processing chemicals are harmful to our health. Often, the best course is to avoid the extremes. Extremes are what kill us.

Diet Action #2: What is one food in your diet that may be harming you? Can you replace it with a more healthful, natural alternative?

~

HEALTHY SUBSTITUTIONS

Despite our best efforts to adhere to a strict diet, sometimes it is not possible. Maybe you are traveling and can't find good food on the road. Perhaps you are at a dinner party, and you don't want to be impolite. Or maybe the foods you eat are out of stock at the grocery store. For these cases, you must learn the art of substitution.

When I was growing up, I loved to drink whole milk. Then people started telling me to drink skim milk because it's healthier. After drinking whole milk all those years, skim milk tasted like tainted water. Eventually, my mother started buying 2% milk. It tasted about the same, so I got used to it. Then she started buying 1% milk. That tasted about the same as 2% milk, so I got used to it. Then, finally, she began buying skim milk. The skim milk tasted about the same as the 1% milk, and I got used to it. The moral of this story is, don't change too much at once. You will have better success in changing your diet if you make small substitutions, one item at a time.

Here are a few substitutions you can consider in your diet:

- Milk → unsweetened almond milk
- Meat → tofu
- Bread → whole wheat bread
- Soda → sparkling water
- Fried foods → baked foods
- Juice → water
- Sugary cereals → muesli

Many items on this list may seem obvious. But keep in mind that there is almost always a healthier option for any food you eat. You might opt for a broiled salmon instead of a burger. But was that salmon farm-raised or wild-caught? Even if it was wild-caught, how fresh is it and was it prepared healthfully?

Even if you're eating the healthiest version of each ingredient, people disagree on what is healthy and what is not. It varies between people and goals. A bodybuilder might tell you soy is bad for you, while a vegan might say otherwise. One nutritionist might say coffee is good, while another might say it's bad. Depending on your genetic makeup, eating wheat can sustain you, or it can make you weak. You know your body the best. Make changes one substitution at a time and see if you feel better or worse.

Diet Action #3: What food do you eat often? Is there a healthier version of that food? Maybe it's time to upgrade your diet.

~

PICK A DIET, ANY DIET

Americans spend over $65 billion a year on weight loss (Marketdata Enterprises, 2017). A search for diet books on Amazon.com shows more than 194,000 results. Despite all the advice and spending, Americans still struggle with their weight.

It's not that the advice is wrong or doesn't work, it's that people are terrible at following diets. Let me tell you a secret. *Every diet works.* You just have to pick one and carefully follow its instructions. Your diet might not work if you combine more than one diet. Your diet won't work if you fudge the rules. Your diet definitely won't work if you don't stick with it.

"Adherence" is the most important word in dieting. When choosing a diet, pick one that you think you can adhere to. A vegetarian diet won't work for you if you crave steak. Likewise, a vegan diet won't work for you if you hate eating your veggies. The most effective diet in the world won't help you lose weight if you refuse to follow it.

Pick a diet you can stick with long-term. Try to find one you can live with for the rest of your life. If the diet doesn't live up to that high standard, then there's no point in starting it. You will only lose whatever progress you've made once you quit.

Here are a few diets that I've either tried with success or look interesting to me:

Diet Action #4: Try the Slow-Carb Diet. This is my favorite diet. The goal of the Slow-Carb Diet is to help your body shed fat while maintaining muscle. In a nutshell, you quit almost all sugars and starches. Meals consist of meat, vegetables, and beans with water as your drink. One day every week, eat whatever you want. For more details, go to www.tim.blog/2012/07/12/how-to-lose-100-pounds.

Diet Action #5: Try the DASH Diet. According to *U.S. News & World Report*, the DASH Diet is the best diet (http://health.usnews.com/best-diet). "DASH" stands for "dietary approaches to stop hypertension." It is based on creating a healthy eating pattern to lower blood pressure. For more information, visit www.nhlbi.nih.gov/health/health-topics/topics/dash.

Diet Action #6: Try the Paleo Diet. Dr. Loren Cordain developed the original Paleo Diet. The premise is that many human diseases did not exist during the Paleolithic times because our diets were different back then. Dr. Cordain advocates eating mostly seafood and lean meats, with some fruits, vegetables, nuts, and seeds. Learn more at his website, www.thepaleodiet.com.

Diet Action #7: Try the Ornish Diet. In this diet, you lose weight by reducing carbohydrates and avoiding fats. The diet allows you to eat all the vegetables, fruits, beans, grains and legumes that you want. You can also have a little low-fat dairy. You avoid all meats, sugars, oily fruits and nuts. To prevent hunger, eat small frequent meals. Exercise and avoiding alcohol is also an essential part of this diet. You can find more information at www.ornish.com/proven-program/nutrition.

Diet Action #8: Try the vegan diet. The vegan diet is simple to understand. Avoid all animal products. Obviously, that means you don't eat meat. But it's less obvious that you also avoid dairy products, eggs, honey, and gelatin. An excellent resource for more information is www.vrg.org/nutshell/vegan.htm.

≈

YOUR DIET IS ALL IN YOUR HEAD

A diet is a state of mind more than anything else. It's a set of rules to help you decide what to eat. It's willpower to help you make the right choices. It's faith that sacrifice now will be worthwhile later.

A diet is not something you can pack into a box and sell from the shelves at a store. It really is all in your head. To diet successfully, you need the right mindset. That includes the right habits, willpower, and a bit of stubborn persistence.

You might have tried and failed in the past. I would guess that you failed because you didn't want it bad enough. You don't just wake up one morning and decide to get in the best shape of your life. There's always a trigger. There's always a moment when you realize you're in bad shape and you will no longer sit idly. It's time to do something about it. You have to diet for the right reasons, and the right reasons are always selfish. Dieting for other people doesn't work. You have to decide for yourself that you're out of shape and you're not going to take it anymore.

In practice, dieting comes down to habits. You eat the way you do today because of habit. If you drink a can of soda with every dinner, that's a habit. If you drink a cup of coffee every morning, that's another habit. Every choice you make for eating and drinking comes from the practices you've developed over the years. To change your food choices, you have to change your habits.

Habits are hard to change. Sometimes that's a good thing, and other times it's bad. That's where willpower comes in. It takes some measure of willpower to change a habit. If you want to start drinking water with every dinner, you need willpower. Your mind tells you to drink soda, but your force of will tells you to drink water. Which side will win? That's the struggle everyone faces when trying to change habits. It's an internal battle. You must always remind yourself that your will is strong. Meditation and visualization can help here. Do what works for you.

Diet Action #9: Meditate for five minutes before each meal. Strengthen your resolve to eat healthier. Visualize how healthy you will be if you stick with your diet. Be mindful of the food you eat and its effects on your body.

~

HACKS

You can trick yourself into eating healthy. Since habit dictates much of how you eat, you can hack your diet by throwing some roadblocks in front of bad habits. Here are a few hacks you can try for short-circuiting your bad eating habits:

Diet Action #10: Eat the healthiest foods first. Most meals include several different dishes. Instead of going for the appetizers or tastiest foods first, eat the healthiest foods first. Eat all the vegetables from your plate before moving on to the other stuff.

Diet Action #11: Use herbs and spices for flavor. Most herbs and spices are just strong-tasting vegetables. Use them instead of sugars, oils, salts, and garnishes.

Diet Action #12: Plan meals in advance. You don't make the healthiest decisions when you're hungry. Pack your lunches to work. Decide your meals before you buy food. Make a shopping list before grocery shopping. Look at the menu and decide on what to eat before sitting down at a restaurant.

Diet Action #13: Fast. Fasting is not eating for an extended period. There are all kinds of benefits to fasting, including starving cancer cells. The easiest way to do it is to stop eating once the sun sets. Don't eat again at least until the sun rises. If you want to fast for longer, don't eat again until lunch the next day.

Diet Action #14: Practice mindful eating. Take your time when you eat. Chew slowly. Think about each bite you take. How does your body feel? Are you full yet? When you slow down your eating, you will eat less unnecessary food.

Diet Action #15: Substitute extra veggies for the carbs. Restaurants often serve bread or rice alongside your main dish. To skip the carbohydrates, ask them if you can have vegetables instead. If they want to charge you extra, either accept the charges or see if they can at least give you some extra veggies. If you are on a low-carb diet, the extra hassle or expense will be worth it.

Diet Action #16: Use smaller plates. Dan Buettner, the author of *The Blue Zones*, introduces a simple solution. Use smaller plates. Eating on smaller plates creates an illusion of more substantial portions. It tricks your brain to give you satisfaction with less food.

Diet Action #17: Keep no junk food in the house. We eat what is convenient when we are hungry. The most convenient food is often junk food. Make a rule that junk food is not welcome in your home. You can eat it outside your home, but don't store junk food in your house. Doing this will remove the convenience factor of the junk food. You will eat less of it as a result.

Diet Action #18: Cook for several days at a time. Cook many servings of food at once. Refrigerate or freeze the extra food. Aside from the initial preparation, healthy meals become quick and convenient.

Diet Action #19: Drink a big glass of water before meals. Not only does it make you feel full faster, but it also ensures you drink enough water during the day.

~

SUPPLEMENTS

If you are changing your diet to lose weight, many supplements can help you. While there is no magic pill for losing weight, some supplements work well alongside diet and exercise. Here are a few popular choices:

Diet Action #20: Drink green tea. Epigallocatechin gallate

(EGCG) is a compound found in green tea. Research shows that it increases metabolism. You can get it by taking green tea extract pills or by drinking green tea.

Diet Action #21: Drink caffeinated beverages. There is no conclusive evidence showing that caffeine can help you lose weight, but it makes sense that it can help. Caffeine is an appetite suppressant and appears to increase calorie burning. Be careful though. Caffeine is a drug. Like any drug, it comes with side effects, including jitters and upset stomach. Also be aware that many drinks and foods containing caffeine also contain a lot of sugar that can offset any benefits.

Diet Action #22: Take hydroxycitric acid (HCA). HCA is a derivative of citric acid that is believed to increase metabolism. Garcinia cambogia extract is the most common source of HCA.

Diet Action #23: Try chitosan. Chitosan is derived from the chitin shells of shrimp and other crustaceans. It appears possible that chitosan can help with weight loss, but so far there is no research to back up the claims.

Diet Action #24: Take conjugated linoleic acid (CLA). CLA is found mostly in meat and dairy products. Lab tests have shown some promising effects of CLA for weight loss, but the evidence is still insufficient.

Diet Action #25: Take whey protein. A by-product of cheese production is whey protein. It is an excellent source of protein and branched-chain amino acids (BCAAs). There is scientific evidence showing that the compounds in whey protein may help with weight loss and muscle gain.

~

TOOLS

Diet Action #26: Track your nutrition with apps. MyFitnessPal (www.myfitnesspal.com) and Lose It! (www.loseit.com) are smartphone apps that help you track your food and exercise. Both apps have barcode scanners that make calorie counting much more manageable. They also both have active online communities.

Diet Action #27: Use a food scale. The nutrition information on the back of your food packages is useless unless you know how many servings you're eating. A kitchen food scale comes in handy for portion control and calorie counting.

• • •

Diet Action #28: Make healthy smoothies. The quickest way to get all your nutrition is to throw it all into a blender and drink it as a smoothie. Use a blender to blend up all the fruits and vegetables you need for the day. You can even add sweeteners, powders, and oils to the mix to make your smoothies more palatable.

Diet Action #29: Use a mister and steamer. If you're avoiding fat, use an oil mister while cooking. Using a steamer for cooking can also cut down on the amount of oil you consume.

Diet Action #30: Carry a water bottle around so you can always stay hydrated. Drinking lots of water also prevents you from getting hungry and keeps you alert.

Diet Action #31: Keep a food journal. Most people don't appreciate how much food they eat each day. Keeping a food journal will make you conscious of how much food you eat each day. You can use any notebook as a food journal, but make sure you choose one that you can carry around easily.

Diet Action #32: Get your genome mapped. 23andme (www.23andme.com) offers personal genetic testing at prices that are affordable to most Americans. Once you get your results, you can upload your data to the genetics tool at www.foundmyfitness.com or www.promethease.com for interpretation. It can yield insights on what diet is optimal for you.

~

RESOURCES

Diet Action #33: Read books on nutrition. Here are some popular choices:

- *The 4-Hour Body,* by Timothy Ferriss.
- *Wheat Belly,* by William Davis MD
- *The Obesity Code,* by Jason Fung
- *How Not to Die,* by Michael Greger MD and Gene Stone
- *The China Study,* by T. Colin Campbell and Thomas M. Campbell II

Diet Action #34: Get some good cookbooks and use them:

- *Trim Healthy Mama Cookbook,* by Pearl Barrett and Serene Allison
- *The Keto Diet,* by Leanne Vogel

- *The Whole30*, by Melissa and Dallas Hartwig
- *Well Fed: Paleo Recipes for People Who Love to Eat*, by Melissa Joulwan
- *Forks Over Knives - The Cookbook*, by Del Sroufe

Diet Action #35: Check out these online resources:

- U.S. News & World Report annual best diet rankings, http://health.usnews.com/best-diet
- CDC Healthy Weight, www.cdc.gov/healthyweight/tools
- American Heart Association Healthy Eating, www.heart.org/HEARTORG/HealthyLiving/HealthyEating/Healthy-Eating_UCM_001188_SubHomePage.jsp
- Ketogenic Diet Resource, www.ketogenic-diet-resource.com
- Choose My Plate, www.choosemyplate.gov
- Eat Right, by the Academy of Nutrition and Dietetics, www.eatright.org
- WebMD Diet Resources, www.webmd.com/diet/health-and-diet-get-more-info
- UC Davis Integrative Medicine Ultimate Resource Guide for Plant-Based Living, www.ucdintegrativemedicine.com/2015/03/the-ultimate-resource-guide-for-plant-based-living-2

Diet Action #36: Listen to diet and nutrition podcasts:

- *The Nutrition Diva's Quick and Dirty Tips,* with Monica Reinagel
- *The Paleo Solution Podcast,* with Robb Wolf
- *The Ultimate Health Podcast,* with Dr. Jesse Chappus and Marni Wasserman
- *Optimal Health Daily,* with Dr. Neal Malik
- *The Keto Diet Podcast,* with Leanne Vogel
- *Food Psych Podcast,* with Christy Harrison

Chapter Six

FITNESS

$\mathcal{H}$ow fit are you? Being fit is not about being skinny or having well-defined six-pack abs. Fitness is about how healthy and resilient you are to take on physical tasks. The following three questions will give you an idea of your overall fitness.

One measure of fitness is body fat percentage. You can estimate it at home with a scale that has bioelectrical impedance analysis (BIA). Many gyms offer more accurate methods of measuring body fat. For this exercise, we don't need to be precise. We'll just eyeball it for now.

Question 1: Look at your belly. What do you see?

. . .

Your Answer:

- It's a round mass of fat: 0 points.
- It's not that big, but I don't see any abs: 1 point.
- It's flat with some defined abs showing: 2 points.

Question 2: What happens when you run up the stairs?

Your Answer:

- I can't run up the stairs: 0 points.
- I can run up the stairs, but I'll breathe heavy at the top: 1 point.
- I run and take stairs often without problems: 2 points.

Question 3: How many pushups can you do?

Your Answer:

- Less than 10: 0 points.
- 10-30: 1 point.

- More than 30: 2 points.

Add up all your points and see how you fared:

- 0-2 points: read this chapter now.
- 3-4 points: come back to this chapter later.
- 5-6 points: skip this chapter, you're good.

∾

THE IMPORTANCE OF FITNESS

Diet alone will only get you so far. A diet without exercise will make you "skinny fat." You will be skinny, but the mass you do have will be made up of fat, not muscle. It is also unhealthy. You want to be lean and fit. That's where the exercise part comes in.

There is an adage that holds a lot of truth: diet to lose weight, exercise to gain muscle. To look good and feel good, you need to be fit. Fit means less fat and more muscle. Muscle is not just for men either. Women also look and feel better when they exchange fat for muscle. Some people call it "toning" or "firming." If you're female, don't worry about getting big bulky muscles. You don't have the hormones for it. It also doesn't happen overnight, as much as many men wish it did.

There are many different types of fitness, depending on your goals. Cardiovascular fitness involves the ability of your heart and lungs to provide oxygen to produce energy. Strength training involves building and strengthening muscles. There is also a difference between being "gym fit" and functionally fit. Ideally, you want to be functionally fit. That means varying your exercises daily, maintaining high range of motion, and using your body to get real work done.

Exercise is not easy. If it were, you wouldn't have to read about it in a book, and personal trainers would be out of jobs. It takes special effort and willpower to start a new exercise routine.

Fitness Action #1: Look at yourself in the mirror. Are you as fit as you want to be? If not, what do you want to improve? Set a goal and write it down.

～

REGULAR EXERCISE

Exercise shouldn't be something you fit into your schedule every once in awhile when you have some free time. It should be an essential part of your day. Exercise should be a habit just like brushing your teeth or eating lunch. Most people would never skip brushing teeth or eating lunch. Why would you skip exercise?

Some people might say they're too busy for exercise. That is short-term thinking. You want to live to be a hundred, don't you? Exercise is one of the critical components of health and longevity. Think long-term. Make exercise part of your daily routine. It is something you absolutely must do each day.

If you don't already exercise every day, use this chapter as your guide to forming a new habit. Make a habit of working out every day. Not once a week, every couple days, or when you have time. Every. Day.

You don't need to wear a special exercise suit and drive to the gym for an hour every day. Exercise can be as simple as getting up from your desk and moving around for a few minutes. It is a conscious effort to move your body more than your baseline activity level. What counts as exercise for one person might not be exercise for another. Every person has a different baseline level of activity. For someone who spends eight hours a day sitting in an office cubicle, taking a 15-minute brisk walk is good exercise. But for someone who is on their feet all day, a 15-minute walk is not exercise. It's resting. Find your baseline and do something harder. That is your exercise. A good guideline is that if you break a sweat, then it's exercise. Exercise at least once a day.

Fitness Action #2: Find at least 15 minutes in your daily routine to devote to exercise. Go ahead and schedule it on your calendar. Then decide what exercise you like to do. It can be as strenuous as a high-intensity workout, or as light as walking your dog. Exercise intensity is relative.

~

PHYSICAL CHALLENGES

Everyone suffers. There is no avoiding it.

Think of exercise as a way of controlling your pain. You can live a sedentary life of gluttony and comfort, but eventually, you will suffer the consequences. You may become obese. You may develop diabetes. You may have an accident caused in part by your weakened physical abilities. Something will happen that will cause you pain. The worst part is that you don't know when it will happen.

On the other hand, if you take on physical challenges now, you will be more prepared for those random events. You will suffer less when they happen. You won't develop many health problems that sedentary people have. When you decide to challenge your physical self, you take the pain now to reduce suffering later. And the best part is you get to choose when you take your challenges.

People challenge themselves physically in many ways. Some run marathons. Others set goals. Still others just exercise regularly, making sure they exert themselves and sweat each day.

Completing challenges also brings a new joy to your life. It is a sense of accomplishment that builds confidence for the future. It is the knowledge that you faced a harrowing experience and came out victorious. That is why people run marathons, take part in obstacle races, and compete in sports.

You don't need to run a marathon to challenge yourself. You just need to have a mentality of challenging yourself. Realize that physical challenges make you stronger and prepare you for future obstacles. Don't shrink away from doing things that are safe, but difficult.

Fitness Action #3: Give yourself a 30-day physical challenge. Use a pedometer and walk 10,000 steps a day for a month. Resolve to set a new personal record at the gym. Make a goal of doing 100 push-ups by the end of the month.

Fitness Action #4: Set a big physical challenge for the year. Sign up for a marathon and train for it. Join a sports team and work to lead your team to victory. Set a goal to climb a mountain next summer, then train yourself for it.

∼

FIXING YOUR WEAKNESSES

What do you focus on when you exercise? It is easy to fall into the trap of only doing what you're good at. After all, it's easy. We like to follow the path of least resistance.

While it's good to enjoy your exercise, if you only do the activities you're good at, you don't get as much return on your investment of time. You see, you get the most gains from a new exercise in the beginning when you're not good at it. The benefits diminish over time as you get better at it and the exercise gets more comfortable. For example, if you're out of shape and haven't run in years, you will have a difficult time running a mile. If you force yourself to get out there and run a mile, you will benefit significantly from the experience. However, if you're an experienced marathon runner, going out and running a mile isn't going to give you much benefit. There are diminishing gains as you gain experience in an exercise.

I'm not saying that expert runners shouldn't run anymore. Just realize that they don't get as much benefit for the time they put in. If you want to get the most out of your exercise time, you should focus on the exercises you're weakest at. They are easy to identify. They are most likely those exercises you avoid because they are too difficult, or exercises you have never done before.

Fitness Action #5: Mix things up as you exercise. You

should do exercises you enjoy, but every once in a while, try a new activity. Or resolve to do a few reps of your least favorite exercise during each workout.

∿

BODYWEIGHT EXERCISES

A common excuse for not exercising is not having the right equipment or not being able to go to the gym. Those are just excuses. You don't need anything to get a good workout. All you need is yourself, some time, and some determination. Here are some of the best exercises you can do with no equipment.

Fitness Action #6: Do pushups. Get on the ground, face down. Put your palms on the ground with your arms outstretched in front of you. Your back and legs must be straight with your toes on the ground and knees off the ground. For each repetition (rep), bend your arms so that your elbows go to at least a 90-degree angle. Push back up to your original position.

Fitness Action #7: Do squats. Stand with your feet shoulder-width apart. Reach your arms straight in front of you for balance. Keeping your heels on the ground, squat down as low as you can. Lift yourself back up to your original position. That is one rep.

Fitness Action #8: Go running. This one is about as straightforward as it gets. Just run. If you want to maximize your time, run as fast as you can. If you have no space to run, you can run in place. Run at least until you break a sweat.

Fitness Action #9: Try the 7-Minute Workout. Scientists have concluded that seven minutes and a chair is all you need to get an excellent high-intensity workout (https://well.blogs.nytimes.com/2013/05/09/the-scientific-7-minute-workout/). Do as many as you can of each of the following exercises, in order, for 30 seconds each:

1. Jumping jacks
2. Wall sit
3. Push-ups
4. Abdominal Crunch
5. Step-up onto chair
6. Squat
7. Triceps dip on chair
8. Plank
9. High knees running in place
10. Lunge
11. Push-up and rotation

12. Side plank

Allow up to five seconds between exercises to catch your breath and set up for the next one.

~

HACKS

There are a lot of little tricks you can do to fit exercise into your day and make it more enjoyable. Here are a few of my favorites.

Fitness Action #10: Start tiny. Start with a laughably easy workout. Just one minute of exercise. Each day, add a minute. By the end of the month, you'll be doing 30 minutes of exercise a day.

Fitness Action #11: Exercise while watching television. Exercise during each commercial break. Or choose something that frequently happens during a movie and exercise each time it happens, like a drinking game (only with exercises instead of drinks). For example, maybe you decide to do ten push-ups every time someone opens a door in a movie.

. . .

Fitness Action #12: Craft a workout playlist. Make the playlist as long as the duration of your exercise. For example, if you want to exercise for 30 minutes, make a playlist with 30 minutes of music. Doing this lets you work out without looking at your watch.

Fitness Action #13: Do things the hard way. Always take the stairs. Park at the far end of the parking lot. Skip the shopping cart and use a hand basket.

Fitness Action #14: Keep your exercise gear ready to go. Keep your gym bag by the door or in your car. You'll save time and have fewer excuses not to exercise.

Fitness Action #15: Force yourself to do exercises before doing something enjoyable. You have to do ten push-ups before you're allowed to open Facebook. You have to do 50 crunches before you can grab a snack. You're not allowed to turn on the television until you jog for at least 10 minutes. Little rules like these create motivation to exercise.

∽

SUPPLEMENTS

As always, please consult with your doctor before trying a new supplement.

Fitness Action #16: Have a green drink. Exercise can take a lot out of you, including essential vitamins. Taking a green drink like Athletic Greens (www.athleticgreens.com) or wheatgrass juice can be cheap insurance to prevent deficiency of certain vitamins.

Fitness Action #17: Drink a whey protein shake. Take whey protein before and after a strength training workout to improve muscle recovery. It speeds the process of gaining muscle and losing fat.

Fitness Action #18: Take branched chain amino acids (BCAAs). BCAAs are amino acids that regulate protein metabolism. Take them before workouts to keep muscles fueled for endurance. BCAAs are particularly helpful for maintaining muscle energy if you're exercising while fasting.

Fitness Action #19: Take creatine. Creatine is a combination of three amino acids. Taking it supplies fast energy to your muscles. Take 2-5 grams of creatine before and after workouts to build muscle mass.

Fitness Action #20: Supplement with beta-alanine. It is a non-essential amino acid that helps reduce muscle fatigue while exercising. It is frequently taken with creatine to provide more energy and endurance during strength training.

Fitness Action #21: Take vitamin D. Vitamin D is an essential nutrient that your body naturally produces when you expose yourself to sunlight. Most people these days have some level of vitamin D deficiency because they spend most of the time indoors. If you don't spend a lot of time outdoors, you will benefit from vitamin D supplementation.

Fitness Action #22: Take fish oil for its omega-3 fatty acids. It reduces inflammation in the body, reducing recovery times and soreness from workouts.

Fitness Action #23: Take glutamine. It is an amino acid that helps you retain muscle mass. It found naturally in nuts, red meats, fish, and beans. If it's not practical to eat a wholesome post-workout meal, supplement with glutamine for a quick fix.

~

TOOLS

Although you can get fit using only your body and bare hands, having exercise gadgets and fitness tools often makes it more fun. Here are a few tools that can make it easier to motivate yourself to exercise.

Fitness Action #24: Use a Fitbit or other fitness tracker. Fitness tracking wristbands today not only measure the number of steps you take but also monitor your heart rate and sleep.

Fitness Action #25: Exercise with kettlebells. Kettlebells are like cannonballs with handles attached to them. They are similar to dumbbells, but much more versatile. Swinging kettlebells makes for a workout that is a combination of strength training and cardiovascular training.

Fitness Action #26: Use a foam roller. Deep tissue massages are helpful for breaking up adhesions and relieving muscle soreness. You won't always have the time or money to get a deep tissue massage after every workout. That's where foam rollers can be helpful. A foam roller lets you massage your muscles by yourself with many of the benefits that a deep tissue massage will give you.

Fitness Action #27: Wear wireless headphones. Many people avoid exercise because they find it both difficult and boring. A good set of wireless headphones won't make exercise easy, but it will at least make it less boring. Play your favorite music, audiobooks, or podcasts and go exercise.

Fitness Action #28: Work out with resistance bands. It's not practical to bring kettlebells with you when you travel. Resistance bands are as small and light as a pair of socks. You can use them to perform a wide variety of strength training exercises.

∾

RESOURCES

Fitness Action #29: Browse an online fitness database.

- Runner's World Race Finder (www.runnersworld.

com/race-finder) makes it easy to find running events near you.

- Exercise Prescription (www.exrx.net) is a comprehensive database of exercises, fitness calculators, and articles. Its database features over 1,600 exercises, each with descriptions and a video demonstration.
- Jefit (www.jefit.com) has a searchable database of over 1,300 exercises and 3,800 workout routines.

Fitness Action #30: Join a branded fitness group.

- Spartan Race (www.spartan.com) is one of the most popular obstacle races. There are many types of Spartan Races varying in difficulty and distance.
- Zumba (www.zumba.com) is an exercise fitness program developed in the 1990s by a Colombian dancer. It is a combination of dance and aerobics set to energetic Latin music.
- CrossFit (www.crossfit.com) is a fitness regimen that combines a high-intensity exercise philosophy with competitive sport.

Fitness Action #31: Read books about fitness.

- *The 4-Hour Body*, by Timothy Ferriss, features uncommon workout routines for maximizing results and minimizing time spent at the gym.
- *Kettlebell - Simple & Sinister*, by Pavel Tsatsouline, teaches everything you need to know to get started with kettlebells.
- *No Gym Needed*, by Lise Cartwright, outlines several exercises you can do at home with minimal or improvised equipment.

Fitness Action #32: Listen to fitness podcasts.

- Ben Greenfield Fitness, with Ben Greenfield (www. bengreenfieldfitness.com), gives you an entertaining mash-up of ancestral wisdom and modern science to optimize your fitness.
- The Fat-Burning Man Show, with Abel James (www.fatburningman.com), has answers and interviews with thought leaders to transform your body, mind, and life with cutting-edge science and practical wisdom.
- The Model Health Show, with Shawn Stevenson, breaks down complex health issues and makes them easy to understand and overcome.

Fitness Action #33: Read fitness blogs.

- Nerd Fitness (www.nerdfitness.com) is a fitness site for regular people who have a day job and can't spend hours at the gym.
- As its name suggests, Men's Fitness (www.mensfitness.com) features articles about fitness for men.
- The Fitnessista (www.fitnessista.com) is another popular fitness blog, but geared towards women.

Chapter Seven

SOCIAL SKILLS

*Y*ou deal with many people over the course of a day. You interact with family, send e-mails, make business transactions, and answer phone calls. In each of your interactions, your social skills determine the outcome.

One common measure of social skills is Emotional Quotient (EQ). It measures emotional intelligence (EI) similar to how Intelligence Quotient (IQ) measures general intelligence. EQ is a measure of how well you can recognize your own and other people's emotions. There are a few tests you can take to assess your EQ, but they are beyond the scope of this book. For this book, estimate your level of EQ by answering the following simple questions:

. . .

Question 1: Is it easy for you to make new friends?

Your Answer:

- Making friends is hard: 0 points.
- I'm average when it comes to making friends: 1 points.
- Making new friends is easy for me. I have lots of friends: 2 points.

Question 2: How well can you read other people's nonverbal cues?

Your Answer:

- I have trouble understanding people: 0 points.
- I'm average: 1 point.
- I'm good at reading people: 2 points.

Question 3: How well do your boss, coworkers, and clients like you?

. . .

Your Answer:

- I don't have many allies at work: 0 points.
- I am well-regarded: 1 point.
- I am a rockstar at my job: 2 points.

Add up all your points and see how you fared:

- 0-2 points: read this chapter now.
- 3-4 points: come back to this chapter later.
- 5-6 points: skip this chapter, you're good.

~

THE IMPORTANCE OF RELATIONSHIPS

Relationships form the foundation of our society. The way we interact with those around us and how we treat each other has an enormous impact on the quality of life we live. In fact, one of the most common regrets among the elderly is that they should have spent more time building relationships and less time working. If you build good relationships, you are more likely to lead a satisfying life.

To build solid relationships, you need to have solid social skills. It doesn't matter if you're introverted or extroverted. How you recuperate your energy isn't a factor in developing social skills. Like any skill, it's all about your technique and practice.

There are many facets to the broad category of social skills. It encompasses personal relationships, interactions with strangers, business negotiations, public speaking, and many others. How you handle interactions with other people will determine what you get out of them.

Like with any skill, you hone social skills by learning the techniques and practicing. This chapter will teach you some of the methods. It's up to you to get outside of your comfort zone and practice them. Practice your social skills by joining groups, volunteering, participating in activities, and otherwise going where people gather. It is not a skill you can practice alone.

Social Skills Action #1: Get out more. Make it a point to get out of your house at least once a day and go somewhere where there are other people. Have at least one interaction with another human being every day. It can be as simple as buying a cup of coffee or sitting next to a stranger at the park.

∼

CONFIDENCE

Confidence is what separates leaders from followers. People will only listen to those with confidence because it shows that they are sure of their message. Confident people are not always right, but they always feel that they are right. They are sure of it. And when people sense confidence in someone else, they are more likely to agree with what they say.

Confidence is difficult, if not impossible to fake. Your microexpressions and verbal nuances give away any lack of confidence that you have. Your voice may quiver. You may unknowingly glance around or shift in your position. Your stress levels rise as you struggle to maintain composure. That is why lie detector tests are so reliable. Unless you genuinely believe in what you say, your body will betray your lack of confidence.

The natural way to gain confidence is by getting enough experience so that you are sure of yourself. But there are also ways you can accelerate the process of building confidence. Here are some tricks:

Social Skills Action #2: Look the part. When you know you look like someone who knows what they're doing, you will start to feel like you know what you're doing. Dress and groom yourself like someone who knows what they're doing. Stand tall. Smile. Taking care of the superficial is the closest you will come to faking confidence.

. . .

Social Skills Action #3: One part of confidence is experience. The other part is knowledge. While you can't take shortcuts with experience, you can with knowledge. Learn as much as you can about your subject. You will instantly be more confident.

Social Skills Action #4: Take 20 minutes to visualize yourself being confident. Envision yourself in a positive situation where everything is going well.

Social Skills Action #5: Slow down. Speak slowly and assertively. Rushing creates the appearance of nervousness. Doing things slowly and deliberately creates the illusion that you're sure of yourself even when you're not.

Social Skills Action #6: Take care of yourself. Get plenty of rest and take time out to exercise.

∾

COMPROMISE

We are all unique. We each have different thoughts from one another. Because of this fact, we will disagree with each other on how to do things.

Answers are rarely black and white. For most problems, there are many solutions, but you must choose one. It is easy if you're the only person making the decision, but things get tricky when more than one person is involved. It becomes necessary to compromise.

The business word for compromise is "negotiate." Because when you compromise, you are negotiating, and when you negotiate, you are compromising. Even if you "win" a deal, you are compromising. The other party will remember. Karma will kick in. Your next deal will not come so easily.

When we compromise, we take a win-lose situation and attempt to make it a win-win. It is a way of optimizing a solution so that it provides the most benefit possible for everyone involved. Here are a few techniques for reaching a compromise:

Social Skills Action #7: Decide on your non-negotiables. You cannot compromise on certain things if you want a good result. Understanding your constraints is the first step in finding an optimal solution.

· · ·

Social Skills Action #8: Find the middle ground and adjust from there. For example, a negotiation over property can begin with an even split of the property. An even split may not be the best solution, but it's a fair starting point for negotiations.

Social Skills Action #9: Trust in karma. Sometimes, the best solution is to give up more than you receive. The other party may recognize that you made a sacrifice and be more willing to work with you on the next interaction.

Social Skills Action #10: Ask a neutral party to mediate and make the final decision. The neutral party should have no interest in the outcome. She should be a respected person known for being fair.

~

COMMUNICATION

Communication is a two-way street. You can speak or write, but that is not communication. You can listen or read, but that is also not communication. You have to both deliver a message and receive feedback for it to be communication. While you communicate, you go back and forth. You deliver your message, then wait for feedback. Then you assess the feedback and give your response.

People judge you by how you communicate. That includes verbal and visual factors, and sometimes elements appealing to the other senses. It is a fact that people think more highly of you if you look and smell good. Those are the passive factors in communication. The active factors include what you say, how you say it, what you do while saying it, and how you listen.

Communication is a set of skills that you can improve with knowledge and practice. Here are a few things you should be mindful of when communicating:

Social Skills Action #11: Respect the person you are speaking with. People can sense it if you talk down to them. Remember that we are all human beings.

Social Skills Action #12: Keep your body language in mind while you communicate. What are you doing with your hands? Are you shifting your feet? Are you making any facial expressions? What is your posture?

Social Skills Action #13: Be conscious of unnecessary conversation fillers and verbal tics. Do you say "um" or "like" a lot? Are there words you overuse? Replace them with thoughtful pauses. It will make you appear more confident.

Social Skills Action #14: Make eye contact. It helps build a stronger connection and shows other people that you are paying attention to them. Similarly, put away distractions like your phone and give the person your full attention.

Social Skills Action #15: Stay positive. Nobody likes to listen to whining and complaining. They also don't want to feel threatened when speaking with you.

Social Skills Action #16: Listen and don't interrupt. Listen to what the other person is saying because you expect the same from them. Keep an open mind and try to see things from their perspective. Pay attention not only to what they are saying but also the non-verbal cues like facial expressions and body language.

~

INTEGRITY

Everyone wants to surround themselves with people they trust. People will only work with others that they trust.

Every relationship is built on a foundation of trust. So if you want to develop any relationship, you first have to build rapport.

The first step to being trustworthy is obvious. Don't lie. When people know you as someone who is not hiding anything, they are more likely to bring you into their inner circle.

When you don't lie, people will respect you. It follows that the next step to being trustworthy is for you to respect others. Remember that every person you meet is just another human being. Everyone you meet, whether a world leader, neighbor or homeless person, is another human being just like you. Every person has their own dreams, struggles, and experiences that made them who they are. Every person is somebody's son or daughter, mother or father, sibling or best friend. We all share our humanity in common. Respect everyone you meet, no matter their position in the social hierarchy.

Here are a few tips for maintaining integrity and building rapport:

Social Skills Action #17: Show interest in others. People love to talk about themselves. Allow them the chance to talk about themselves, and they will often return the favor.

Social Skills Action #18: Smile. Smiling shows that you are a friend. It allows others to let their guard down because you are not a threat.

Social Skills Action #19: Get the person's name and remember it. Use the person's name when speaking with them.

Social Skills Action #20: Be helpful to others. People will not interact with you if they perceive it as a waste of time. How can you provide value to the other person? Make their problem your problem.

Social Skills Action #21: Give genuine compliments. If something about the other person impresses you, mention it. It's probably no accident. Receiving praise might just make their day.

Social Skills Action #22: Speak slower. It gives you more credibility because it gives people more time to understand what you're talking about.

～

HACKS

Social Skills Action #23: Become a human lie detector. An essential part of social skills is reading people. That includes knowing when someone is lying. While there are no rules that will determine lying with perfect accuracy, you can make a reasonable guess by paying attention to certain things. Here are some things to look out for that may indicate lying:

- A desire to change the subject or shut down the conversation.
- Moving hands to face. Adjusting clothing or nearby objects. Hiding the face or mouth. These fidgety behaviors signal anxiety or desire to obscure indications of lying.
- Carefully scripted responses may be indications of lying or hiding the whole story. Ask the same question three different ways and see how the answers compare.
- Non-congruent gestures like saying "yes" while shaking the head may indicate lies.
- Putting too much thought into answering an easy question. Pay attention to how much time it takes for someone to answer easy questions. "Did you break into my car yesterday?" If the answer comes after some thought, the person may be lying.

None of these are entirely accurate indicators of lying.

Some people are good at lying. Others may act suspicious even when telling the truth because they are anxious. It is essential to establish a baseline for how the person behaves when telling the truth and, ideally, how they act when telling a lie.

Social Skills Action #24: Mirror others to build rapport. Everybody sees themselves as normal. If you want to build rapport with someone, try using their mood, language, and body language as your own. Pronounce words they same way they do. Stand with the same posture. Laugh when they do. They will like you better because you appear to be just like them.

Social Skills Action #25: Master the art of small talk. Keep a script in your head for various topics of conversation. Ask questions, because people love to talk about themselves. Whenever you want someone to elaborate and keep talking, repeat the person's last few words: "That's when I decided to go to Italy." "Go to Italy?"

Social Skills Action #26: Use the "Yes, and..." technique. It is an improv comedy technique where you continue a line of conversation by accepting what the other person said and expanding upon it. It is useful in encouraging free sharing of ideas. For example, "Guns should be kept out of schools." You might reply, "Yes, and there should also be metal detectors at every entrance."

~

SUPPLEMENTS

While no supplement can provide you with social skills, some supplements can elevate your mood and reduce anxiety.

Social Skills Action #27: Try SAMe (S-Adenosyl-L-Methionine). SAMe is derived from an amino acid that occurs naturally in every human cell. It is often used to treat depression because it increases serotonin and dopamine production in the body.

Social Skills Action #28: Take Kava root pills. They are generally safe to take as long as you use them as directed. They can reduce anxiety.

Social Skills Action #29: Take omega-3 fatty acids like those found in fish oil. They may reduce bouts of depression. Omega-3 fatty acids are also essential for building brain cells.

. . .

Social Skills Action #30: Try valerian root, which is another ancient supplement that is also helpful for treating anxiety and insomnia because of its sedative effect.

Social Skills Action #31: Take 5-HTP (5-hydroxytrypto-phan). 5-HTP is extracted from an African woody shrub (Griffonia simplicifolia). It is often used to treat ADHD and anxiety.

Social Skills Action #32: Drink chamomile tea. It is a natural way of reducing anxiety.

Social Skills Action #33: Try taking St. John's Wort. It helps your body produce serotonin to combat depression.

Social Skills Action #34: Drink green tea. It has blood pressure and heart rate leveling properties useful for fighting anxiety.

Social Skills Action #35: Take Brahmi (Bacopa monnieri).

Brahmi is a natural nootropic that improves cognitive function. It may also boost motivation and reduce anxiety.

Social Skills Action #36: Try lemon balm, which is often used to ease digestive problems and headache pain. It can also reduce anxiety.

Social Skills Action #37: Take lavender to produce a powerful calming effect that may help relieve anxiety and depression.

~

TOOLS

Social Skills Action #38: Take public speaking courses. Toastmasters International (www.toastmasters.org) is the most well-known public speaking course. It is more of a club than a class. Members go to practice communication skills. Another public speaking course worth looking into is the Dale Carnegie (www.dalecarnegie.com) public speaking course. Billionaire investor Warren Buffett cites it as one of the most life-changing events of his life.

Social Skills Action #39: Use social media. In the United

States, the two biggest social media platforms are Facebook (www.facebook.com) and Twitter (www.twitter.com). Making moderate use of those services can enhance your social life in the online space. However, spending too much time on them will have the opposite effect.

Social Skills Action #40: Use your smartphone. You don't need to be face-to-face with someone to communicate. Remember the primary purpose of your smartphone. Call someone and chat. Skype (www.skype.com) is a good option for video calls. WhatsApp (www.whatsapp.com) might be the most popular messaging app in the world today (2017).

Social Skills Action #41: Use collaboration software. Collaboration software has made the world smaller. You no longer have to be in the same room with someone else to work with them. Popular choices for collaboration software include Slack (www.slack.com), Asana (www.asana.com), and Trello (www.trello.com).

Social Skills Action #42: Try Computer Voice Stress Analysis (CVSA). One tool you can use for helping determine if someone is telling the truth is CVSA. It is not as reliable as a polygraph test, but all you need is someone's voice and the software. Search your device's app store for "voice stress analyzer." IOS users can search the Appstore for the Agile Lie Detector app.

Social Skills Action #43: Keep a gratitude journal. A lot of times, the thoughts and worries you have stuck in your head are the cause of your anxiety. Writing down the things you're grateful for can reduce stress by forcing you to think of the positive things in life.

Social Skills Action #44: Try a local hookup app. If you're looking for romantic relationships, dating apps like Tinder (www.tinder.com) or Coffee Meets Bagel (www.coffeemeetsbagel.com) can help you find a date. If you just want to find friends and socialize, try Meetup (www.meetup.com).

~

RESOURCES

Social Skills Action #45: Visit websites that teach how to improve social skills.

- *Improve Your Social Skills* (www.improveyoursocialskills.com) is a comprehensive online guide to social skills.

- *Succeed Socially* (www.succeedsocially.com) is a free online guide to getting past social awkwardness.
- *The Accidental Negotiator* (www. theaccidentalnegotiator.com) is a blog written by a professional negotiator about how to use sales negotiation and persuasion skills effectively.
- *The Urban Dater* (www.theurbandater.com) is a blog about online dating, relationships, and sex.

Social Skills Action #46: Listen to podcasts about social skills.

- *Social*, with Jason T. Rogers, helps you become a better communicator.
- *The Art of Charm*, with Jordan Harbinger (www. theartofcharm.com), will make you a higher performer, a better networker, and a deeper connector.
- *How to Talk To Girls Podcast*, with Tripp Kramer, provides dating advice for men.

Social Skills Action #47: Read books on social skills. The following is a big list of books that are either very popular or that I have read and got a lot out of. I've included their full titles so you can look up the ones that appeal to you most. They are listed in no particular order:

- *Influence: The Psychology of Persuasion,* by Robert B. Cialdini
- *How to Win Friends and Influence People,* by Dale Carnegie
- *How I Raised Myself from Failure to Success in Selling,* by Frank Bettger
- *Mate: Become the Man Women Want,* by Tucker Max and Geoffrey Miller
- *Confident You: An Introvert's Guide to Success in Life and Business,* by S.J. Scott and Rebecca Livermore
- *No More Mr Nice Guy: A Proven Plan for Getting What You Want in Love, Sex, and Life,* by Robert A. Glover
- *The Game: Penetrating the Secret Society of Pickup Artists,* by Neil Strauss
- *What Every BODY is Saying: An Ex-FBI Agent's Guide to Speed-Reading People,* by Joe Navarro and Marvin Karlins
- *How to Talk to Anyone: 92 Little Tricks for Big Success in Relationships,* by Leil Lowndes
- *The Charisma Myth: How Anyone Can Master the Art and Science of Personal Magnetism,* by Olivia Fox Cabane
- *The Definitive Book of Body Language: The Hidden Meaning Behind People's Gestures and Expressions,* by Barbara Pease and Allan Pease

- *Spy the Lie: Former CIA Officers Teach You How to Detect Deception,* by Philip Houston, Michael Floyd, Susan Carnicero, and Don Tennant
- *Never Split the Difference: Negotiating As If Your Life Depended On It,* by Chris Voss and Tahl Raz
- *Just Listen: Discover the Secret to Getting Through to Absolutely Anyone,* by Mark Goulston and Keith Ferrazzi

Chapter Eight

ORGANIZATION

*Y*our organizational skills are reflected in your reliability and neatness. Well-organized people are more reliable than those of us who leave clutter in our wake. You can count on them to remember appointments and arrive on time. They stay on top of things. They finish what they start before moving their focus to other things. Can people rely on you? How organized are you?

Question 1: How often do you arrive late to appointments? Do you ever miss appointments? Do you arrive unprepared?

Your Answer:

- I have trouble being on time and frequently don't have time to prepare adequately: 0 points.
- I am late or unprepared occasionally: 1 point.
- I am always on-time and prepared: 2 points.

Question 2: How does your work area look?

Your Answer:

- It's a war zone. I can never find anything in the mess: 0 points.
- It's cluttered, but functional: 1 point.
- It's neat and clean: 2 points.

Question 3: How do your work and personal projects usually go?

Your Answer:

- I rarely finish a project: 0 points.
- Projects occasionally go past deadline or over budget: 1 point.

- Every project I work on is on-time and within budget constraints: 2 points.

Add up all your points and see how you fared:

- 0-2 points: read this chapter now.
- 3-4 points: come back to this chapter later.
- 5-6 points: skip this chapter, you're good.

∽

THE IMPORTANCE OF ORGANIZATION

People want to understand things. They want to have control. Organizing your possessions is one way to have more understanding and control over your life.

Organization is a form of abstraction. Abstraction is taking a complicated concept and simplifying it. For example, a car has hundreds of parts. Most of the time, you don't need to think of the individual components of the vehicle. You just refer to the product as a whole. It's a car.

Organization works the same way. You take a big pile of stuff, separate it all out, and put each item away. Pens go into a pen holder. Office supplies you don't use every day go into the drawer. Books go onto the bookshelf. You don't need to worry about each item. You can take solace in the fact that if you need any book, you can find it on the bookshelf. Being organized saves you time because you know where each item should be.

A good organization habit makes it easier to do tasks. Meetings get scheduled with reminders. You know where to find your tools when you need them. You can easily locate any file that a client requests. You know what task you need to do next to complete your project.

It's all about the systems you put in place to ensure that everything that needs to get done gets done.

Organization Action #1: Do an organization audit. What parts of your workspace, home, and life are the most cluttered? Write down the five areas that you need to organize the most.

~

YOUR TIME

What do you do now? If you're organized, you know exactly what you need to do at any given time. Most people are not so organized. Most people spend a lot of time deciding what to do next.

The time you spend between tasks is called overhead. If you want to do more each day, you need to reduce the overhead as much as possible. It might seem like a productivity problem, but it is an organization problem. If you spend a lot of time between tasks, you need to organize your day better.

There are a few ways to make your day more efficient to reduce overhead. One way is batching. Take a task that you do several times a day or several times a week, and consolidate it to fewer times. If you do laundry three times a week, can you do larger loads once or twice a week instead? If you check email throughout the day, can you check it once in the morning and once in the afternoon instead?

Organization Action #2: Make a list of things you do more than once a day. Can you do each of those things only one time a day? Make another list of things you do more than once a week. Can you find a way to do each of those things just once a week?

Another tactic for keeping your schedule manageable is saying no. If you say yes to every request and invitation, your schedule will quickly fill up with other people's agendas. It will become an unmanageable mess of unproductive meetings, events you don't want to attend, and tasks assigned to you by others. You will lose focus and miss meetings. Despite considerable efforts, you will become unorganized and unreliable.

There is a place for taking every opportunity that you come across. But once your career is underway and you have clear goals to focus on, you need to say no to anything that will take you off track. As entrepreneur Derek Sivers said, "No more yes. It's either HELL YEAH! or no." Fill your schedule with things you're excited about. Say no to everything else.

Organization Action #3: For every opportunity you come across, ask yourself if you're excited to do it. If you're not thinking, "Hell yeah!", then you should decline the opportunity.

~

YOUR WORK AREA

When you were little, your parents probably nagged you to clean up your toys after you were done playing. They were teaching you a valuable life lesson. You could be as messy as you wanted while you were playing, but once you were done, you had to clean up your mess.

Business researchers have proven it time and again. People working in neat work areas get more work done. The work they do is better. The truth is, your workspace is a reflection of your work.

Creativity is a chaotic process. When you're in "the zone," things can get out of hand. Creativity is disorganized, and the act of being creative will lead to a cluttered workspace. That's okay. But it's also important to clean up after the creative work is done. If you don't, the dust will never settle, and the disorganization will continue into your essential non-creative work. It is why many creative people have trouble finishing projects. They let the chaos of initial creation spill into the later phases of their project like design, production, and marketing. When the entire project is a work of chaos, it never gets completed.

Cleaning up your workspace serves as a reset for the project. You can sit back, look at your bare desktop, and start your next work with a clean slate. Literally. It will get messy again, especially when you get inspired. Do your work, clean up the mess, and repeat. Just like when you were little.

Organization Action #4: Clean up your work area after finishing each task. Don't start the next task until the mess from the previous task is cleaned up.

~

YOUR DIGITAL LIFE

If you are under 25 years old, you've probably spent your entire life with the internet. The internet has created an alternate reality that runs parallel with the real world. Chances are, if your real-world life is cluttered and disorganized, your digital life is as well.

How many media files do you have stored on your computer and phone right now? That's pictures, videos, documents, and audio files. At one point, I had over 20,000 photographs, hundreds of video clips, hundreds of documents, and 2,000 MP3 music files sitting on my computer. I also had over 3,000 bookmarked articles that I was planning on reading eventually. You might have a similar problem with digital clutter. Let's be honest. I was never going to sort through the almost 30,000 media files sitting on my computer. The solution to the digital clutter problem is not more storage. The answer is better curation.

Fortunately, we have two tools that will tame your digital mess: the 80/20 rule and the cloud.

The 80/20 rule was developed by Italian economist Vilfredo Pareto after he observed that about 20% of the peapods in his garden contained about 80% of the peas. Since then, people have found the phenomenon almost everywhere. For our purposes, we can assume that 20% of your media collection will receive 80% of your attention. You will probably not miss the other 80% of your media collection if you simply deleted it.

Organization Action #5: Use the 80/20 rule on your digital files. Go through your files and pick out the 20% that are most important. Archive or delete the rest.

. . .

"The cloud" is a fancy term for "internet storage." You don't have to store anything on your computer or phone anymore. You can save it to Dropbox, Google Drive, Apple iCloud, YouTube, Flickr, or any of the other myriad of cloud storage platforms out there. That means I could store my 30,000 media files on the cloud and delete them from my hard drives.

The magic happens when we use the 80/20 rule together with the cloud. I can think of two approaches:

Organization Action #6: Back up all of your files to the cloud. Then go through and delete 80% of them from your hard drive. That way you never really delete anything, but you have your most important files physically stored on your device (and also backed up).

Organization Action #7: Go through your media files and choose the best 20% to back up to the cloud. This way you also don't delete any files, but the most important ones are backed up in cloud storage.

~

YOUR PROJECTS

If you want your projects to succeed, you need to organize them well from the beginning. Planning is crucial. A project with no clear starting point, path, or goal cannot succeed.

When planning a new project, start with the end in mind. What product do you want to have after all the work is done? Once you know that, you can start working backward to define the project's path and the starting point.

Define the goal of your project. What are your expectations? When is the deadline? What is your budget? Who are the stakeholders, what resources do you need, and who do you need to hire? Come up with a name for your project.

After your goals and expectations are worked out, you need to come up with an execution plan. What needs to get done before you can reach your goal? For this portion of the planning, you may want to brainstorm with other people involved in your project.

Break down the goal into several small tasks. Assign due dates for each job to be completed. What are the milestones and when should you reach each of them? Can you break each task into todo lists of even smaller tasks? If you're working with other people, make sure each person knows their role and associated deadlines.

Once you know your goals and how to get there, the final planning step involves getting started and receiving feedback. How will your team communicate with one another? How often will meetings occur? How will team members be held accountable? What happens if there are problems or delays?

Organization Action #8: Get a pencil and paper. Brainstorm your next project. Answer all the questions above. Write down whatever comes to your head. The act of getting your ideas down on paper will help define your project and provide a clear path for moving forward.

Organization Action #9: Plan for disaster. Have a separate brainstorming session to plan for obstacles. Every project will hit some snag along the way. List everything that could go wrong, then write down some solutions for each problem.

~

HACKS

Organization Action #10: Use the 43 Folders System. It is a tickler file system that consists of using a filing cabinet with 43 folders to get through your work. You can learn more about it from the YouTube video, How to Create and Use the 43 Folders System (www.youtube.com/watch?v=YG0FU_M_YB8).

. . .

Organization Action #11: Use mind mapping to organize your thoughts into a cohesive document. A mind map a picture you draw on paper with each of your ideas from brainstorming. Start by drawing the main topic in the center of your paper and circling it. Write down every thought you have and draw a line coming out of the part of the map that inspired that thought. For more details on drawing mind maps, watch How to Mind Map with Tony Buzan (www. youtube.com/watch?v=u5Y4pIsXTV0)

Organization Action #12: Use the 1-3-5 Rule. Each morning when you wake or on the night before, write down your one biggest task for the day. Then write down three small tasks that you would like to complete. Then write down five other tasks that are not as important, but would be nice to complete if you have time. Start your day by doing the biggest task. Don't move to the other tasks until your biggest task is complete. Then work on your three smaller tasks and don't move on to the other five until those three are complete.

Organization Action #13: If you're working with a team, make sure everyone uses the same software. It's a pain in any organization if people are using different software apps. Get everyone on the same page with the same software: word processors, messaging apps, and project apps. Not only should the software be the same, but everyone should also run the same versions.

Organization Action #14: Use desktop organizers. The saying, "a place for everything, and everything in its place" applies here. Make sure everything in your work area has a place, whether it be a box, a drawer, or a designated spot on the desktop. When you work, always put things back where they belong after you're done with them.

Organization Action #15: Use group file storage. Have storage space in the cloud where the entire team can access the work files. Doing that will remove the need for having a mess of different versions of the same files scattered all over the network.

~

SUPPLEMENTS

As you might have guessed, there are no supplements you can take to improve your organization skills or to tidy up your office for you. However, organization extends to all areas of life. A disorganized person can become disorganized with the supplements they take. You can quickly go crazy with supplements. Some supplements are best taken on an empty stomach, while others on a full stomach. Others require timing intervals between doses throughout the day.

One way to keep your supplements in order is to simplify. Instead of keeping track of ten different pills, see if you can take combination supplements.

Organization Action #16: Take multivitamins. For those who don't have the time or desire to research supplements, multivitamins are an excellent choice. According to Labdoor (www.labdoor.com), the best multivitamins are:

- Garden of Life Vitamin Code for Men
- Garden of Life Vitamin Code Perfect Weight
- Nature's Way Alive Max Potency Multivitamin
- Rainbow Light Men's One
- Garden of Life Vitamin Code for Women

Organization Action #17: Eat nutrition bars. Replace your pantry full of sweet and salty snacks with boxes of protein bars. They are much healthier snacks than a bag of potato chips or cookies. Labdoor recommends these five protein bars

- Quest Bar
- Premier Protein

- RXBAR
- thinkThin High Protein Bars
- MET-Rx Protein Plus Bar

Organization Action #18: Take meal replacements. Rather than throwing together a rushed meal at home or having junk food on the go, try a meal replacement. Labdoor recommends these:

- Vi-Shape
- Herbalife Formula 1
- Vega One All-in-One Shake
- Labrada Lean Body
- Soylent

~

TOOLS

Organization Action #19: Manage your projects with software. The internet has changed the way we organize our work. Sure, we can manage projects the old-fashioned way with paper and secretaries. But that's time-consuming, tedious, and results in stacks of paperwork that nobody wants to look through. In this regard, technology has made life easier. These days, we have project management software. Here are some of the more popular choices:

- Asana (www.asana.com) is a web and mobile application that helps teams track projects from start to finish.
- Trello (www.trello.com) is a web-based project management application that uses boards, lists, and cards to help teams collaborate, organize, and prioritize projects.
- Basecamp (www.basecamp.com) a web-based project management tool that features to-do lists, milestone management, forum-like messaging, file sharing, and time tracking to organize projects all in one place.
- Zoho (www.zoho.com) is an online office suite featuring more than 35 separate applications for running your projects.
- G Suite (gsuite.google.com) is a set of cloud computing apps developed by Google. It includes Gmail, Hangouts, Calendar, Google+, file storage, document editing, spreadsheets, slides, forms, websites, and interactive whiteboard.
- Microsoft Office (www.office.com) is an office suite of applications, servers, and services developed by Microsoft for creating, communicating, and collaborating on projects.
- Slack (www.slack.com) is a powerful collaboration

tool that allows people to share messages, conversations, and files.

Organization Action #20: Use digitization tools. The paperless office used to be a dream. Today, the dream has come true. It is finally possible to have a truly paperless office. You need a computing device connected to office software like Microsoft Office or Google G Suite. You also need either a scanner or smartphone to digitize documents. On smartphones, Evernote (www.evernote.com) is a popular app that helps you digitize your documents.

Organization Action #21: Use a file cabinet and folders. If you work better on paper, go with the time-tested organization approach. Get a file cabinet with hanging folders. Label your folders and keep all your documents organized. You can even use the 43 Folders System (described in Organization Action #10) to keep your work files in order.

Organization Action #22: Use a desktop organizer. If your desktop is often cluttered, you need a desktop organizer. A desktop organizer creates a place for each item on your desk so you can quickly find things while you work and clean up after you work. Search "desktop organizer" on your favorite online retailer's website to see the possibilities. Or if you have some money to spend, check out the modular system developed by Ugmonk (www.ugmonk.com/gather).

Organization Action #23: Use a calendar. Get a physical or virtual calendar. The benefit of a physical desk calendar is that it is always in sight so you can see your day's tasks at a glance. Virtual calendars are useful for editing your schedule from anywhere and setting up reminders to alert you of appointments.

Organization Action #24: Use cloud apps. Cloud storage apps keep your files on the internet so you can access them from anywhere and from any device. Dropbox (www. dropbox.com) and Google Drive (drive.google.com) are two popular choices.

∼

RESOURCES

Organization Action #25: Listen to organization podcasts:

- *Organize 365*, with Lisa Woodruff, supplies home organization tips, strategies, and motivation.
- *Organize Your Life*, with Clutter Coach Claire,

provides ideas so you can get organized and stay that way.

- *Project Management for the Masses Podcast,* with Cesar Abeid, helps project managers take their lives and careers to new levels.
- *The Minimalists Podcast,* with Joshua Fields Millburn and Ryan Nicodemus, discusses living a meaningful life with less.
- *Optimal Living Daily,* with Justin Malik, features audio articles on personal development, minimalism, productivity, and more.

Organization Action #26: Read books on organization:

- *The Life-Changing Magic of Tidying Up: The Japanese Art of Decluttering and Organizing,* by Marie Kondo.
- *Essentialism: The Disciplined Pursuit of Less,* by Greg McKeown.
- *Real Life Organizing: Clean and Clutter-Free in 15 Minutes a Day,* by Cassandra Aarssen.
- *Sink Reflections: Overwhelmed? Disorganized? Living in Chaos? Discover the Secrets That Have Changed the Lives of More Than Half a Million Families,* by Marla Cilley
- *Simplify,* by Joshua Becker

Organization Action #27: Read blogs on organization:

- No Sidebar (www.nosidebar.com) is a blog about getting rid of the excess and focusing on the essentials.
- Be More With Less (www.bemorewithless.com) is about simplifying your life and really living through decluttering and focusing on the best things.
- IHeart Organizing (www.iheartorganizing.com) is run by a mother of three, who shares tips on maintaining an orderly home despite a busy family life.
- Unclutterer (www.unclutterer.com) is a website for home and office organization featuring tips, organization strategies, product reviews, reader questions, and more.
- Creating Mary's Home (www.creatingmaryshome.com) offers advice for creating happier, more peaceful, more functional homes.

Chapter Nine

PERSONAL FINANCES

*M*oney doesn't solve all your problems, but it does reduce worry. Your goal should be to accumulate enough wealth so that you don't need to worry about what happens if you lose your job, or if you will have enough money in old age, or if you can put food on the table and a roof over your head. According to a 2010 study by Princeton University's Woodrow Wilson School, increases in income make you happier up to a certain point. Once you reach about $75,000 a year, further increases in income won't make you any happier. Answer these questions to determine how you're doing with your finances:

Question 1: How long could you go on living your current lifestyle if you lost your primary source of income today?

. . .

Your Answer:

- Less than a month: 0 points.
- Two to six months: 1 point.
- More than six months: 2 points.

Question 2: What's the trend in your net worth?

Your Answer:

- I'm poorer this year: 0 points.
- My net worth is about the same this year as last year: 1 point.
- I'm getting richer every year: 2 points.

Question 3: Would your life change drastically if you suddenly had $1 million wired into your account?

Your Answer:

- My life would be completely different: 0 points.
- I'd make a few changes: 1 point.
- Not really: 2 points.

Add up all your points and see how you fared:

- 0-2 points: read this chapter now.
- 3-4 points: come back to this chapter later.
- 5-6 points: skip this chapter, you're good.

~

THE IMPORTANCE OF PERSONAL FINANCES

At its core, money is a record of favors owed. I give you a cabbage from my garden. You give me a dollar in exchange. The dollar is an "I owe you" note. Next month, I can hand you that same dollar and ask for a watermelon in return.

When you work for money, you're doing favors for other people. They give you money in return for the favors. You can then use your money to ask favors of other people. Those favors can be anything that has value: food, services, electricity, entertainment, etc.

To make money, help others. Help as many people as you can, as much as you can. That is the path to wealth.

Your goal when you work is to build enough wealth so

that when misfortune strikes, you can use your money to ask favors of others. Beyond a certain amount, money ceases to improve your lifestyle. Sure, you can always pay for more lavish goods and entertainment, but it doesn't really improve your life. And enjoyment is relative. Once you get used to a lavish lifestyle, you cease to enjoy the simpler things in life.

The Millionaire Next Door by Thomas J. Stanley and William D. Danko distinguishes between prodigious accumulators of wealth (PAW) and under accumulators of wealth (UAW). If you want to become a millionaire, you need to be a PAW. That means making lots of money while spending significantly less than you earn. It's the ratio between the two that matters. If you make $50,000 a year, but only spend $20,000 of it, then you are a PAW. If you make $500,000 a year but spend it all, then you are still a UAW.

Be a PAW. Eventually, you will become a millionaire.

Personal Finances Action #1: Get a pen and paper. Write down how much income you make each year. Then figure out about how much you spend each year. Are you a PAW or a UAW?

TRACKING YOUR CASHFLOWS

As Peter Drucker once said, "what gets measured, gets managed." He also said, "if you can't measure it, you can't improve it." Both of these quotes were said in the context of business, but also apply to your personal finances. After all, your personal finances are the business of **you**. If you track your finances, they get managed. If you can measure your finances, you can improve them.

Personal Finances Action #2: You don't need fancy software to track your finances. Just create a new spreadsheet in your favorite spreadsheet app. If you don't have a spreadsheet app, use Google Sheets (sheets.google.com) because it's free. You can get sophisticated with your tracking, but for now, just use two columns. On the left column, write down the name of each expense you have. On the right column, write the amount of money you spent on it. Track every single penny you spend for at least a month. At the end of the month, review your expenses. Most people doing this are shocked to see all the little things they mindlessly spend money on. You will probably spot a bunch of items that are unnecessary. Tracking every penny you spend will make you aware of where your money is going. And being aware will allow you to manage and improve your finances.

. . .

Look at money not as numbers, but as streams. You have a stream of money coming in (your income), and a stream going out (your spending). Your streams are your cashflows. To improve your finances, you will want to make your income stream as large as possible, while making your spending stream as small as possible. You will also want to increase the number of income streams you have, so you're safe if one stream dries up (like if you're laid off from your job). Similarly, you should decrease the number of spending streams by canceling your unused services and stopping unnecessary purchases.

Personal Finances Action #3: Take 15 minutes and brainstorm ways you can increase the amount of money you make in a year.

Personal Finances Action #4: Take 15 minutes and brainstorm ways you can reduce spending each year.

∿

BE ON THE LOOKOUT FOR OPPORTUNITIES

Opportunities are everywhere. The smarter you are and the more you know, the more opportunities you will see.

Learn as much as you can about the world around you.

You can do it by reading or by going out and doing things. Or you can do both. Learning puts the seeds of ideas into your mind. Those seeds will make you aware of opportunities when you see them.

You've already missed out on millions of opportunities. But they will keep coming. If you miss one, just learn some more and be on the lookout for the next one. There will always be a new opportunity for smart people like you to notice. Only those who have stopped learning ever feel trapped with nowhere to go.

You might have heard about the Law of Attraction. You probably dismissed it as pseudoscience and woo-woo. And you were right. It is a pseudoscience, and it is also a whole lot of woo-woo if you take it at face value. I mean, how can daydreaming about your bank account filling up with a million dollars make it happen? Yes, that part of the Law of Attraction is fantasy and a lazy distortion of the original concept. Here is how the Law of Attraction really works: when all you think about all day every day is making a million dollars, you will notice every opportunity around you for making a million dollars. Take advantage of the Law of Attraction by spending all of your time learning about, daydreaming about, and taking action on achieving your goals. You will notice that opportunities are everywhere.

Personal Finances Action #5: Write down the thing you want most in the whole world. How much do you want it?

How much time you spend on something should be proportional to how much you want it. Start spending more time on the thing you want most to make the Law of Attraction work for *you*.

~

INVESTING

Warren Buffett, possibly the greatest stock market investor who ever lived, once outlined his rules of investing:

- Rule #1: Never lose money.
- Rule #2: Never forget rule #1.

Buffett's investing rules might be oversimplified, but they describe the core of investing in three words. Never lose money. Notice that it doesn't mention making money. Investing is not about wealth *generation*. It's about wealth *preservation*. As I described earlier, you make money by helping as many people as you can, as much as you can. Once you get your money, you hold onto it by investing it.

If you live in the United States, your cash devalues by 2-4% every year. That is called inflation. 2-4% might not sound like much, but consider the long-term effects of inflation.

Suppose you know nothing about investing. You just became a proud parent, and you want to save money for your child to go to college. You look up the tuition and see that it costs $10,000 a year. So you do what any parent with no knowledge of investing might do. You put $10,000 in cash into a big trunk and bury it in your backyard in the dead of night.

Fast-forward eighteen years later. Your daughter just graduated from high school and was accepted to college. You dig the nest egg up from your backyard. The $10,000 in cash is still there. You bring it to the college bursar's office where you make a heart-sinking discovery. Tuition had gone up over the past 18 years. It now costs $18,000 a year. Inflation caused the prices of everything to increase, and the value of your cash to decrease.

How do you avoid the ravages of inflation? By investing your money. If the parent who did not know about investing had put the $10,000 into the stock market, that money would probably be worth over $55,000 after 18 years. That's because the average annual return from the S&P 500 stock market index is about 10% a year.

When you invest your money, as long as you make money faster than inflation devalues it, you will never violate Rule #1. Don't forget that.

Personal Finances Action #6: Learn everything you can about investing and invest your savings.

～

RUNNING YOUR OWN BUSINESS

By definition, businesses sell products and make profits. That's all you need to have a successful business. At least one product. A profit. That's it. Let's look deeper into those two crucial components of a successful business.

A product is something that someone else wants. If somebody wants it, it's a product. If nobody wants anything your business produces, your business will fail because you don't have a product. How do you know if people want something you create? By testing the market. Preferably, you test the market before you spend your time and resources creating something. Test the market by asking potential customers if they would buy the product if it existed. Create a prototype and show it to people. Gauge their interest. Are they willing to give you a down payment so that they will be the first to have the product when it's ready? Listen to the people who put their money where their mouth is.

Personal Finances Action #7: Think about different products that you can sell to others. Do you know how to make something that other people enjoy? You could sell it. Are people always asking you for help because you have a specific skill? You could provide it as a service.

Once you have a product, you're halfway toward having a

successful business. Now you need a profit. Profit is what you have left over when you take all the money you made from customers and subtract all of your expenses from making the product available. If you're not making a profit, you need to either charge more money for your product or decrease the costs of producing the product. Or you could do both. Make it easier on yourself and make sure you're profitable from the start. Set your prices high. It's easy to lower your prices later, but difficult to raise them without hard feelings from your customers. Don't spend money you don't have to make your product. In the beginning, create a minimum viable product as cheaply as possible. You can always add features later. You can always upgrade your equipment later. Reinvest all your profits, but not more, back into your business.

Personal Finances Action #8: Create a minimum viable product (MVP) and try selling it. An MVP is a product with the minimal set of features. But don't forget the "V" in "MVP." Your minimal product must still be viable. The one feature it has must be worth paying for. Try selling it. If people like it and it's profitable, you can add features and scale up production. At that point, you have a business.

∽

HACKS

Personal Finances Action #9: Automate your finances. Set up automatic deposits for all your income and automatic payments for all your bills. It makes for less worry and less chance you'll forget to pay your bills on time.

Personal Finances Action #10: Reduce dependence on others. If you can do things yourself, do them yourself. At least until you get on solid financial ground, you should do as much as you can yourself. Stop paying people to cook your food, trim your bushes, and clean your home. Do those chores whenever you have free time. It won't be easy or enjoyable, but you'll thank yourself later when you're financially independent.

Personal Finances Action #11: Simplify your accounting. Cut back to the bare minimum in services and credit cards. It's much easier to keep track of one or two credit cards than seven.

Personal Finances Action #12: Transfer your debt. If you're struggling with credit card debt, find a credit card that will give you a 0% interest introductory offer. Do a balance transfer to move your debt from your highest interest credit cards to the new 0% interest credit card. That should buy you some time to pay down your debts without racking up vast amounts of interest.

Personal Finances Action #13: Use only cash. Credit cards don't feel like real money. But if you carry bills and coins around to pay for everything, you keep a better sense of what you are spending when you buy things.

Personal Finances Action #14: Go minimalist. You don't have to do anything extreme. Just resolve to get rid of two old things for every new thing you buy. Eventually, this habit will get you down to your bare minimum. Another rule of thumb to keep in mind: if you haven't used something in over a year, you probably don't need it.

~

SUPPLEMENTS

Personal finance is a mental game. Therefore, the supplements that will help you most are nootropics, or smart drugs. Here are some of the more popular ones. Keep in mind that I am not a doctor and this list is for informational purposes only. Not all of these drugs are legal everywhere, and some require a doctor's prescription and supervision. Do your own research and consult with a medical professional before trying any of these.

Personal Finances Action #15: Try piracetam. Manufactured in the 1960's, Piracetam is the original nootropic drug. It has been researched and used for over 50 years and is considered safe and non-addictive. Piracetam has been found to improve memory, verbal learning, and focus. It has a low incidence of mild side effects including headache and gastrointestinal upset. It is also relatively cheap compared to other smart drugs.

Personal Finances Action #16: Try Noopept. Noopept is over 500 times more potent than Piracetam. Like piracetam, it is capable of enhancing memory, learning, and focus. Noopept is also a powerful antioxidant that prevents neurological disorders and helps the brain grow. Because of this, it is thought to improve long-term memory.

Personal Finances Action #17: Take Modafinil. Modafinil is a prescription drug that is known to increase focus and problem-solving abilities. Users report that it promotes motivation and concentration, resulting in higher productivity. It is not addictive, but regular users can develop a tolerance for it.

Modafinil is also expensive. It costs $500-$900 for a 30-day supply.

Personal Finances Action #18: Try adrafinil. For all the effects of modafinil without a prescription, there's adrafinil. Adrafinil is a precursor to modafinil. When you take adrafinil, your liver converts it to modafinil after about an hour. The main drawback is that it taxes your liver and can cause an elevation in liver enzymes.

Personal Finances Action #19: Take aniracetam. Aniracetam is the only member of the racetam family of drugs that also has a stress-lowering effect. It is known to boost memory, cognitive ability, and confidence levels. Many people use it before stressful events such as public speaking or tests. It is often used with choline to prevent the primary side effect of headaches.

~

TOOLS

Personal Finances Action #20: Track your finances with Mint (www.mint.com). Mint is a free website that helps you track and manage your finances. It is owned by Intuit, the makers of TurboTax and QuickBooks.

. . .

Personal Finances Action #21: Manage finances and business operations with Airtable (www.airtable.com). It is online software that is a cross between a spreadsheet app and a database. You can easily add photos, contact information, priority levels, and checkboxes to indicate completion. Real-time collaboration features allow you to comment on files and share information with your team.

Personal Finances Action #22: use ProductHunt (www.producthunt.com) to find trendy new products before the rest of the world finds out about them. ProductHunt introduces the best new products daily. Products they recommend include apps, websites, books, and technology.

Personal Finances Action #23: Browse AngelList (www.angel.co). It is an interface between startup companies and the rest of the world. You can post jobs for your own startup, find startup jobs, or invest in startup companies.

Personal Finances Action #24: Invest with TD Ameritrade (www.tdameritrade.com). It is an online brokerage that allows you to buy and sell stocks online.

Personal Finances Action #25: Learn about investing using

Yahoo! Finance (finance.yahoo.com). It offers financial news, a stock portfolio manager, and stock screeners to help you research your next stock purchases.

Personal Finances Action #26: Use Freshbooks (www. freshbooks.com). Freshbooks has small business accounting software that makes it easy for you to send invoices, organize expenses, and track payments.

Personal Finances Action #27: Use PayPal (www. paypal.com) to facilitate online money transfers. With PayPal, you can send or receive money using email addresses or mobile phone numbers.

Personal Finances Action #28: Use Kickstarter (www. kickstarter.com) to gauge interest and fund your product idea before you spend too much time or money producing it.

∼

RESOURCES

Personal Finances Action #29: Read books on personal finances:

- *Rich Dad Poor Dad: What the Rich Teach Their Kids About Money That the Poor and Middle Class Do Not!*, by Robert T. Kiyosaki
- *The Total Money Makeover: A Proven Plan for Financial Fitness*, by Dave Ramsey
- *The Richest Man in Babylon*, by George S. Clason
- *MONEY Master the Game: 7 Simple Steps to Financial Freedom*, by Tony Robbins
- *The Intelligent Investor: The Definitive Book on Value Investing*, by Benjamin Graham
- *The Millionaire Fastlane: Crack the Code to Wealth and Live Rich for a Lifetime*, by MJ DeMarco
- *Secrets of the Millionaire Mind: Mastering the Inner Game of Wealth*, by T. Harv Eker
- *The $100 Startup: Reinvent the Way You Make a Living, Do What You Love, and Create a New Future*, by Chris Guillebeau
- *I Will Teach You To Be Rich*, by Ramit Sethi
- *The Essays of Warren Buffett: Lessons for Corporate America*, by Warren E. Buffett

Personal Finances Action #30: Explore personal finance websites and blogs:

- Mr. Money Mustache (www.mrmoneymustache.com) is about living a frugal, yet "Badass" life of leisure.

- The Motley Fool (www.fool.com) has free articles and podcasts for individual investors. Their flagship products are their premium stock market investing newsletters.
- Seeking Alpha (www.seekingalpha.com) is an investing website featuring curated articles from thousands of contributors.
- Financial Samurai (www.financialsamurai.com) delves deep into investing, real estate, retirement planning, career strategies, money philosophy, and more to help you achieve financial independence sooner, rather than later.
- WiseBread (www.wisebread.com) is a community of bloggers writing to help you live large on a small budget.
- Get Rich Slowly (www.getrichslowly.org) covers a range of topics related to attaining greater financial freedom.

Personal Finances Action #31: Listen to podcasts on personal finances:

- *You Need A Budget (YNAB)*, with Jesse Mecham, is a weekly podcast about getting out of debt, saving more money, and beating the paycheck-to-paycheck cycle.

- *Listen Money Matters*, with Andrew Fiebert and Thomas Frank, offers actionable personal finance advice with a dose of brash humor.
- *The Dave Ramsey Show*, with Dave Ramsey, teaches you how to manage and budget your money, get out of debt, build wealth, and live in financial peace.
- *The Financial Mentor Podcast*, with Todd R. Tresidder, reveals unconventional wealth building advice and advanced investment strategy tips.
- *Wall Street Unplugged*, with Frank Curzio, offers financial news and interviews with leading economists and investment professionals.

CONCLUSION

Life is a daily cycle of challenges. Some of the challenges are predictable, while others seem entirely random. It often seems that whenever life becomes too comfortable, Fate likes to throw a bigger challenge our way. In a way, the problems make it fun to live. They keep our keep our minds working and curiosities piqued. We are challenged each day to solve the obstacles, knowing that if we don't, the problems will continue to fester until we do.

One percent improvement every day. That is my mantra for starting each new day. What new problems will challenge you today? It's like a game. Every problem you solve gives you a surprise reward. Nobody knows the problem you get, and nobody knows the reward. That is part of the joy of living.

I'm nowhere near perfect. I haven't mastered everything,

and I never will. Nobody will. That's because the array of problems to solve and knowledge to learn is infinite. The best we can do is continuously strive to resolve the issues as they arise. It's only when we give up that things spiral out of control and life gets worse for us. Stay in control. You have the power to change any aspect of life.

Compiling the list of actions for this book has made me more aware of my strengths and weaknesses. Especially the weaknesses. Some of the actions I wrote about are a part of my daily routine. But the majority are areas for improvement. They are actions I know I should be taking but for one reason or another, am not. As someone who strives for self-improvement, you likely face the same struggles. Even if you already know about most of the actions in this book, I hope they at least serve as reminders so you can use them in your arsenal of tools for solving whatever challenges life throws at you today.

Life Action #1: Strive to improve yourself by one percent every day.

HAVE YOU JOINED THE E-MAIL LIST YET?

Want to see secret blog posts, get free and discounted books, and get updated content? Join the StormShock e-mail list.

It's free. I'll keep your e-mail secret. Unsubscribe at any time.

Subscribe at www.smshock.com/list

ABOUT THE AUTHOR

Steve Alvest has always had trouble focusing on one thing. He graduated from Virginia Tech with an MBA in information technology, a B.S. in computer science, and minor degrees in history, mathematics, and studio art. During his time in college, he also dabbled in various martial arts, languages, and extreme diets. He has worked professionally in the fields of software engineering and intellectual property law. Steve now writes in the suburbs of Washington, D.C. with his wife, dog, three kids, and about 30,000 baseball cards.

Connect with Steve Alvest online:

Website: www.SteveAlvest.com

E-mail: steve@stormshock.com

ALSO BY STEVE ALVEST

Blog Ideas: 131 Ideas to Kill Writer's Block, Supercharge Your Blog and Stand Out (smshock.com/blogideas)

Summary of Think and Grow Rich: The Wisdom of Napoleon Hill (smshock.com/summarythink)

Summary of How to Win Friends and Influence People: Lessons from Dale Carnegie (smshock.com/summaryfriends)

www.ingramcontent.com/pod-product-compliance
Lightning Source LLC
Chambersburg PA
CBHW051823040426

42447CB00006B/334